THE OFFICIAL HISTORY OF THE
METROPOLITAN
POLICE

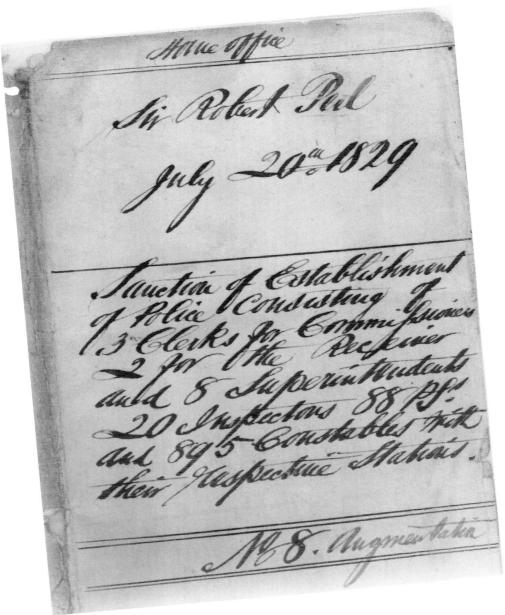

Sir Robert Peel's original instructions establishing the Met Police.

THIS IS A CARLTON BOOK

Design copyright © Carlton Publishing Group 2004
Text copyright © Carlton Publishing Group 2004
Metropolitan Police Crest and Photographs (where stated in the
    Picture Credits) © Metropolitan Police Service

This edition published in 2004 by Carlton Books Ltd
A Division of the Carlton Publishing Group
20 Mortimer Street
London
W1T 3JW

A CIP catalogue for this book is available from the British Library.

ISBN: 1 84442 602 5

Project Co-ordinators: Luke Knight and Caroline Kenyon
Executive Editor: Stella Caldwell
Senior Art Editor: Vicky Holmes
Designer: Simon Wilder
Copyeditor: Ros Lavine
Production: Lisa Moore

THE OFFICIAL HISTORY OF THE
METROPOLITAN
POLICE

GARY MASON

175 Years of Policing London

CARLTON

Foreword

It gives me great pleasure to be able to introduce this fascinating book, which gives an account of 175 years of history of the Metropolitan Police Service.

When I became Commissioner in 2000, I was excited yet humbled by the enormity of the job. Excited, because both the Metropolitan Police and Scotland Yard are famed around the world and occupy a unique place in the history of policing. London is one of the world's greatest cities, a vibrant and cosmopolitan capital that offers a multitude of challenges to the blue light services. There is nowhere else quite like it. But humbled, because there is a strength of history to the Metropolitan Police Service that is unlike almost any other organisation.

The 175th anniversary of the Met is a remarkable milestone in the long and distinguished history of this extraordinary organisation. The Service has changed and grown immensely since the first officers stepped out on to the streets of London in 1829. Neither policing nor crime stands still and the challenges of the 21st century are more than equal to any the Met has faced throughout its history.

The multitude of changes the Met has undergone, and the reasons why, are detailed in this book. But there are two things that certainly have not altered. The first is the principle on which our policing philosophy is based: that all Metropolitan Police staff work for and within the community they are part of, and not an enforcement organisation apart from it. Britain, and London in particular, has given a tradition of firm and fair policing by consent to the world and that is something of which we in the Met are fiercely proud and that we strive every day to uphold.

The second is our commitment to make London safe for all those who live in, work in and visit the capital. As Commissioner, it has been my stated vision to make London the safest major city in the world. This is a considerable task and we are making real progress, but there is still work to be done. We are continually striving to build on our achievements and improve the service we give to the people of London. But, while we are doing so, it is important to stop and remember our history, the lessons we have learnt, and the thousands of stories of courage, brilliance and humanity that have gone before. I have no doubt that future generations of Met officers will still be giving their utmost to pursuing the same aim another 175 years from now.

Writing this foreword also gives me a wonderful opportunity to pay tribute to those people who represent the heart and soul of policing – the officers and staff who do the job. Above all, what makes the Met so extraordinary is its people. We should always be thankful that there are individuals of such courage; the bravest of the brave, willing to risk their lives as part of their everyday duties in the continuing battle against the perpetrators of crime and disorder. At times, I can't help feeling that we take them for granted. Perhaps that's a tendency we have with those nearest and dearest to us. They are the everyday heroes and heroines of this city, doing the most exceptional things in the most demanding of circumstances. Too many of our colleagues have paid the ultimate price in the fight against crime. Every officer who has died in the line of duty is remembered, not only in this book but every year in our Service of Remembrance and every day in our hearts and the hearts of their loved ones.

I am proud to have been the twenty-fifth Commissioner of the Metropolitan Police Service. I hope history will record a worthwhile and positive contribution by the Service and its officers and staff to the people of London. I have confidence that the Met is in good shape for whatever the future may hold.

I hope you enjoy reading this book.

Sir John Stevens QPM DL
Commissioner of the Metropolitan Police

1 The birth of the new police

Social historians are divided as to the true extent of the crime wave that persuaded Parliament to set up the Metropolitan Police in 1829. No crime statistics exist for the period and we rely on eyewitness accounts of London – the 'thieves' kitchen' – at the time, which were readily available for sale as books and pamphlets.

Then, as now, the written word in its popular printed form was a powerful influence on the public's fear of crime. The perception that the streets were lawless and dangerous places played a large part in the acceptance of the necessity of Robert Peel's New Police. John Bee's *A Living Picture of London for 1828* paints a vivid account of a lawless city ruled by violent thieves, con men and unruly mobs. What little policing existed, in the author's view, was inefficient or corrupt and in the pay of organised gangs of criminals. 'Always prefer streets to lanes and these again to narrow alleys and passages especially by night,' Bee warned the reader of his 18th-century guide to the metropolis. Thames Street, Aldgate, Butcher's Row, the Seven Dials and the lower parts of Westminster were 'everyone of them to be avoided by delicate persons of either sex'. 'Ways of the Town', a poem of the period, is even more bloodcurdling:

> *Prepare for death if here at night you roam,*
> *and sign your will before you sup from home*

Left A Met officer poses in the five-button tunic introduced in 1897. This was replaced by a seven-button tunic in 1934.

Watchmen and patrols

As a deterrent, before Sir Robert Peel's 1829 Act, policing existed only as an amorphous collection of parochial and often unpaid parish constables, watchmen and patrols. Bee was largely dismissive of watchmen and constables who 'looked on' while women were forcibly kidnapped in the street and 'suffer well known thieves to mix in the crowds'. Many of these early guardians of law and order were clearly corrupt, taking their share of the booty while gangs of thieves 'prowl up and down under the patronage of the watchman'.

But not all early forms of policing in the capital were as ineffective or corrupt as authors and essayists like John Bee described. In 1798, marine police had been established to tackle the huge problem of corruption and theft from merchant ships among seamen, dockers and customs officers who worked in the Port of London. Patrick Colquhoun, a merchant and magistrate, founded the service jointly with former sailor John Harriott. With the help of funding from the Treasury and the West India Company, 220 constables were employed, assisted by 1,000 registered dockers who were hired to load and unload vessels legitimately.

The constables did not wear uniforms but were heavily armed, and they had an immediate deterrent effect. In the first year of operation of the marine service, more than 2,000 offenders were found guilty of offences committed on the river. Colquhoun's and Harriott's river police are widely regarded to be the first police service in the world in the sense that they were not government-controlled but were responsible for the prevention and control of crime. The marine police were merged into the Metropolitan Police in 1839 as Thames Division – a name it kept until 2004 when it was re-branded the Marine Support Unit.

The uniformed Bow Street foot and horse patrols, which started operating from Bow Street Magistrates'

Court in 1805, were equally organised and committed. They acted as a genuine deterrent to criminals and were a prototype to the permanent police service eventually established by Peel's Act of Parliament. These patrols are often mistakenly referred to as the 'Bow Street Runners'. Established by Henry Fielding in 1753, the Runners were, in fact, the first organised detective service and were paid a retainer and often a reward on capture for the arrest of criminals wanted by the magistrates. They didn't wear uniforms, but carried short tip-staves with gilt crowns as a mark of their authority. The Runners were also very low in number, comprising only eight men.

The Bow Street patrols of the early 1800s were a far more visible deterrent. The 52-strong horse patrol, established by chief magistrate Richard Ford in 1805, wore bright red waistcoats and were armed with pistols, handcuffs and truncheons. Their impact was immediate, earning them the nickname 'Robin Redbreasts'. A year later a Bow Street foot patrol was added to the ranks and by 1821 its number had been increased to nearly a hundred men.

Robert Peel's new police

Sir Robert Peel, who became Home Secretary in 1822, had championed the Bow Street patrols and one of his first acts in office was to introduce a uniformed day patrol to supplement the Service's regular patrols at night. Peel was a strong advocate of crime prevention rather than harsher punishments for those found guilty of misdemeanours. He was also keen to find a way of maintaining public order without the need for military intervention. In the years leading up to his appointment there had been regular bouts of violent disorder and protest on London's streets, which culminated in the Queen Caroline riots in 1821. Caroline was the exiled wife of the very unpopular King George IV who had tried to divorce and depose her. When she died and her body was taken through the streets of London to Harwich, a huge mob converged on the funeral procession to voice its anger. The Bow Street police, escorting the procession, were heavily outnumbered and eventually troops fired into the crowd, killing two people.

When he came to office Peel set to work at once by

Above left Watchmen getting ready for their shift at Marylebone Watchhouse in 1808. The public often regarded such patrols with scepticism.

Above right Sir Robert Peel, the founding father of the New Police, was keen to find a way of maintaining public order without the need for military intervention.

setting up a select committee, with himself as chairman, to review the policing arrangements for the capital. But the committee was not convinced by the new Home Secretary's arguments and rejected the concept of a professional police service. Undeterred by this setback, Peel set up another select committee in 1828 which recommended the establishment of a new service. The Metropolitan Police Act 1829 gave authorisation to two executive magistrates to establish a single service covering an area of seven square miles.

Two commissioners were appointed, Colonel Charles Rowan and Richard Mayne, a barrister, who were given free rein to establish the service as they saw fit. A building to serve as headquarters was rented in Great Scotland Yard off Whitehall. The original strength was 895 constables, 88 sergeants, 20 inspectors and eight superintendents. Within a year Rowan and Mayne had recruited a force of more than 3,000 men organised into seven divisions.

The recruitment criteria were that that the men had to be under 35, in good health, strong and at least 5 ft 7 in (1.7 m) tall. Peel's model for the New Police was that they were to be mainly a crime prevention service, not heavily armed and highly visible to dispel any notion that they were a quasi-military body in the pay of the government. The uniforms worn by the men were carefully chosen to emphasise the civilian nature of their role. Stovepipe hats – an early version of the tall

helmets worn by Met officers ever since – and blue swallow-tail coats marked them out in the crowded streets. Most officers only carried truncheons for personal protection and rattles as a means of calling for assistance. The hats were reinforced with cane stays and were strong enough for officers to stand on to look over fences. The collars of the uniforms were strengthened with leather straps to protect the constables from garrotting – then a common form of attack by criminals.

Nevertheless, the New Police quickly became known as 'Peelers' and 'Bobbies'. Neither of these nicknames were terms of affection. They alluded to the fact that the commissioners and the receiver of the Metropolitan Police were answerable directly to the Home Secretary – and there was a perception that Peel had effectively created his own private service. However misguided the public's view of this was, these terms of reference proved to be significant.

Until July 2000 – with the creation of the Metropolitan Police Authority (MPA) – the Met was the only police service in the UK that was answerable directly to the Home Office with no formal means of local accountability.

Citizens in uniform

So who were the first Metropolitan officers and what motivated them to take on such a difficult and dangerous job? Money was hardly the main attraction. The wage of one guinea (£1.05p) a week was about the same as that of a farm labourer.

Some of the early Met officers certainly came from military backgrounds and accepted the military-type discipline imposed by Colonel Rowan. Despite his adherence to tried and tested methods of drilling,

Left An officer pictured in traditional 'Peelers' uniform which was worn from 1829 until 1864. Note the high, strengthened 'anti-garrotte' collar and stovepipe hat.

me-ting with good support

square-bashing and army-style rigour, Rowan proved to be an inspired choice in moulding this new civilian service. He stayed faithful to Peel's blueprint of a non-paramilitary body of men whose main purpose was to be highly visible on London's streets and prevent crime. In setting out the rank structure, the Commissioner carefully avoided the use of military nomenclature. With the exception of sergeant, all the supervisory officers took on administrative titles, such as inspector and superintendent. The Service's 'foot soldiers' were constables – a public office familiar to the English population for centuries.

A General Instructions book was laid down, emphasising the virtues of calm, self-restraint, civility and respect for civil rights. The first Met officers were not allowed to frequent public houses, talk to prostitutes, associate with known criminals or cultivate them as informants. Modern officers would view these instructions as ludicrous and counter-productive but there were sound reasons for having such a rigid code of personal conduct. First, the corrupt association between criminals and the early constables and watchmen was still a source of public scandal. Peel's new service could have died at birth if full-time, paid police officers had been viewed by the public as being no better than the amateur grafters who had gone before. Second, excessive drinking in early Victorian London was a serious social problem, not least among public officials. Rowan's zero-tolerance approach to drinking on duty proved to be a prescient move. Within two years of being established, more than half the Met's manpower had been sacked for drink-related offences and absenteeism and had been replaced. The police officer allocated Warrant Number 1 was dismissed for drunkenness after only four hours as a policeman.

Nevertheless, Peel's New Police, in terms of tackling

Above From the time of the Metropolitan Police's formation in 1829, the new 'Peelers' were an outstanding success. By the turn of the century recorded crime had fallen dramatically.

the lawlessness that had brought about its formation, was an outstanding success. From 1830, London's population grew by a fifth every decade so that by the turn of the century it had reached more than six million people. In the same period, recorded crime, as measured against each 1,000 head of London's population, fell dramatically. By 1900 there were fewer offences reported than when the Metropolitan Police had been established 70 years earlier even though the population had grown by about five million people during that time. When it was formed, the Metropolitan Police had about 3,000 men policing a population of 1.5 million. By 1899 there were 16,000 officers and the population of London had grown to seven million.

The Metropolitan Police Act of 1839 gave officers substantial new powers to control pubs, vagrancy, betting shops, theatres, street markets and prostitution. But then, as now, such establishments and the social interaction that revolved around them were part and parcel of everyday life in the city. London had quickly become the biggest port in the world, with a teeming itinerant population. Policing by consent required a subtle system of police control rather than a draconian application of the letter of the law.

Peel's service did not use its extensive new powers to close down or drive out establishments that attracted miscreants and petty criminality but acted to control the crime in their vicinity. In this way an important social contract was established between police and public that contributed to the Met's success in preventing crime.

Throughout those first seven decades of the Met's existence the total number of recorded crimes for the Metropolitan Police District (MPD) never went much above 20,000. To set that against the modern era, the total number of offences recorded in the MPD in 2003/2004 stood at more than one million. One hundred years earlier, the Commissioner of the metropolis was able to sleep soundly at night. With 12,000 officers available for duty to police an area of 688 square miles, crime per 1,000 head of population had been falling steadily for 25 years. In his annual report for 1892, Sir Edward Bradford was able to boast that the crime rate in London had been halved in 20 years. Of the 85,000 people arrested by the police that year, more than 30,000 were for drunkenness. The figures for manslaughter were the lowest since records had begun. There were 637 burglaries and 1,320 cases of housebreaking in that year but only four of these offences involved any violence.

As impressive as these figures are, there was nothing particularly scientific about the policing methods employed. The vast majority of officers in the early Met patrolled a system of interlocking beats on foot. Two or three times during their eight-hour shift they would have to report to their sergeant at a prearranged point on the beat – a sort of mobile clocking-in system. Vigilance and acting to prevent

Above This *Punch* cartoon published in 1881 entitled 'An unequal match' reflected public concern that unarmed constables were no match for criminals who carried firearms.

crime in a highly visible way was the mainstay of the beat officer's work, most of which was solitary and monotonous, but effective.

On December 22, 1899 the *Police Review and Parade Gossip* – a magazine founded seven years earlier to promote the welfare and improvement of professional police officers – interviewed a London beat officer at 6 a.m. just as he was coming off night shift. The officer, who did not want to be named, told the reporter that his first duty after 10 p.m. was to go around every house in every street on his beat to make sure householders had closed their windows and doors. Any large houses which would be particularly attractive to burglars merited closer attention.

'I fasten a piece of black thread across the outer gates when I pass around 11 o'clock and if, when I pass again at 12 the thread is intact, I know that no one has been through,' the constable confided. 'The same applies to back and side entrances. By this simple method many a crafty housebreaker has been caught red-handed. I suppose that no city in the world is so carefully guarded during the night as London.'

Early grievances

The low crime rates and homespun craft of the constables should not detract from the fact that they regularly faced danger from determined criminals who often carried firearms, even for routine offences such as burglary. Debates about whether the Metropolitan Police should be armed commenced soon after the force was established and continue to this day.

PC Joseph Grantham was the first officer to be murdered on duty. He was kicked to death while trying to intervene in a fight between two drunken men in Somers Town, near King's Cross, on June 29, 1830. Tragically PC Grantham died the day after his wife gave birth to twins. Unbelievably, the coroner's jury verdict into the killing concluded that PC Grantham had brought about his own death by 'over exertion in the discharge of his duty'. Since that first murder, names of officers killed in the line of duty have been steadily added to the Met's Roll of Honour, and public and press sympathy for the policeman's lot has ebbed and flowed with each fresh outrage. In 1881 PC Frederick Atkins was shot three times and killed when he disturbed a burglar during a routine visit to a large house on his beat in Kingston on the outskirts of the MPD. A reward of £100 for information leading to the capture of the killer was offered but the assailant was never traced. More than 1,500 officers were present at PC Atkins's funeral and newspaper editorials drew attention to the dangers faced by unarmed constables patrolling remote beats without any protection or back-up.

A year later PC George Cole was shot in the head and killed while attempting to arrest a burglar in

Dalston. The severe wounding of PC Patrick Boans a year later by armed burglars in Wimbledon prompted a sea change in police and public attitudes. The *Evening Standard* published an editorial on August 29, 1883 calling for a radical reappraisal of the Met's policy on carrying firearms. 'It is not only foolish but absolutely cruel to send policemen out to combat men possessed with revolvers without any other arm than a short club,' it thundered.

A cartoon of the time in *Punch* magazine entitled 'An unequal match', which depicted an officer grappling with a burglar who is armed to the teeth, summed up the mood. The then Met Commissioner, Sir Edmund Henderson, was stung into action and conducted a survey of all officers serving in London's suburbs. More than two-thirds asked to be issued with revolvers. In a letter to the Home Secretary the Commissioner asked permission to 'issue revolvers to such men as desire to have them when employed on night duty in the exterior districts and who can... be trusted to use them with discretion'. In July 1884, more than 900 officers were issued with revolvers and authorised to carry them on night duty. The regulation permitting officers to carry weapons on night duty on the outskirts of the MPD remained in force until 1936 but, in fact, the practice had almost died out by the turn of the century.

Facing armed criminals alone with only a short wooden stick for protection was bad enough, but there were more deep-rooted grievances that affected officer morale. Pay was poor and to earn it officers had to work seven days a week without a rest day. An average shift lasted up to 12 hours, performed in two phases. Although officers were supplied with uniforms and boots, the latter were loathed for their lack of comfort – a significant grievance when they were walking up to 20 miles a day. It wasn't until 1897 that Met officers were granted a boot allowance so they could buy their own.

This, allied to a rigid discipline system, fuelled officers' sense of injustice. The wastage rate for officers in the early years of the Met ran at more than 33 per cent per year. There was also an undercurrent of resentment about the 'officer class' – often from military backgrounds – who more often or not were drafted straight into the highest ranks, while lower- and middle-ranking officers were subject to a rigid bottom-up promotion system. Eventually, a hierarchy was established in the Metropolitan Police on the basis that all senior officers had to rise through the ranks, a principle that survives to this day. But the autocratic style of many of the Met's early commissioners and their assistants – former generals and majors to a man – convinced many officers that those at the top had little empathy with the rank and file.

A report in *Police Review and Parade Gossip* in 1885 alludes to 'signs of increasing discontent amongst the London Police'. It accused the Met's 'semi-military organisation' of acting as a powerful safeguard against officers being able to air their grievances. 'Discipline has been carried to such a pitch, we are told, that a man was lately fined for turning his head the wrong way at drill. A general order has been issued which forbids any section of the force to meet together. It is clear that the enterprising constable who would complain of his lot must gang warily and avoid anything like publicity which is regarded in official quarters as a sort of treason.' But the editor's harshest comments were saved for those at the top. 'The clerical department at Scotland Yard is considered to be very much over-staffed and the four chief constables with salaries of £800 per annum each and various privileges, might it is said, be very well dispensed with.'

The growth of trade unions and the Labour movement, with the emergence of socialism as a political force, also encouraged more militant attitudes among police officers. The lack of a pension scheme or a representative body through which Met officers could push for better working conditions fanned the flames. Met officers had won higher wages after 180 of them across four divisions refused to report for duty in 1872, but three of the ringleaders were jailed and more than a hundred were suspended.

In 1890, 39 striking officers were dismissed after troops were called in to restore order outside Bow Street when socialist sympathisers joined a crowd of protesters to show solidarity with the men. The strikers' main grievance – the lack of a negotiating body for the police – was ignored. The introduction of a pension for police officers in 1890 and a weekly rest day in 1910 could not assuage the clamour for a police trade union.

At the end of the First World War in 1918 the top rate of pay for a Metropolitan PC was 48 shillings a week, about half that of an engineering worker. Many Met officers with families had to rely on charity to clothe and feed their children or 'moonlight' by taking other jobs. The prospect of a serious police strike had been building up for decades and in 1918 it happened, with 6,000 Met officers out of a total strength of 18,000 walking out. Despite the

Right Met officers have kept public services going in times of industrial unrest. The sensitive policing of the General Strike in 1926 won widespread public support.

ominous signs of discontent among the ranks, the strike shocked the government of the day under Prime Minister Lloyd George.

Overnight, Lloyd George increased police pay and pension entitlements, encouraged the resignation of Commissioner Sir Edward Henry and established a Royal Commission to investigate the pay and conditions of police officers. The Desborough Committee was appalled at the poverty levels of many police families and found that some officers were suffering from malnutrition. It reversed the unskilled labour tag that had been established 90 years earlier by Sir Robert Peel. Met officers were now semi-professional men in terms of their salary and pension entitlements. 'We are satisfied that a policeman has responsibilities and obligations which are peculiar to his calling and distinguish him from other public servants and municipal employees,' it said. The committee's recommendations also led to the creation of the Police Federation in 1919, not a trade union but a powerful

negotiating body established on a statutory footing.

The Police Act of that year may have given the Met's rank and file the representative voice they had long fought for but it also enshrined significant restrictions on their power as a united labour force. Under the Act, officers were prohibited from joining any trade union or taking an active part in politics. It also became a criminal offence to induce a police officer to go on strike. Since that Act came into force, Met officers have been present at many industrial disputes but their role has been to break up illegal picketing and prevent disorder and unlawful assembly. This has sometimes led to violent confrontations between police and striking workers, notably at the Grunwick strike in 1978 and the Wapping printers' dispute in the mid-1980s. Met officers have also kept public services going in times of industrial unrest, such as during the General Strike in 1926, and in disputes involving other emergency services like the fire brigade and ambulance staff. The Service also played a crucial co-ordinating role in housing remand prisoners in police cells during a long-running industrial dispute between the Prison Officers' Association and the Home Office in the 1980s.

Equal opportunities

If the period leading up to the First World War was significant in improving the pay and status of London's police, the war itself had an even greater impact on the future make-up and organisation of the Service. With large numbers of Met officers enlisted in the armed forces, imaginative ways of filling the manpower gap were actively sought by the Home Office and police hierarchy. One method was to establish the Metropolitan Police Special Constabulary as a

Left War time Special Constables parade in gas masks. These volunteer police officers proved a vital stop-gap for the large number of regular officers conscripted into the armed forces.

permanent force of volunteers in 1915. Until that date, part-time volunteer officers had been sworn in and given powers of arrest but only in times of civil emergency such as riots and illegal demonstrations. With a significant proportion of the Met's normal peacetime strength fighting in France, Specials were now given uniforms and took over routine policing duties like beat patrols.

During the Second World War, Specials played a more significant role in policing the capital as they were allowed to volunteer for full-time duties and be paid. Their numbers were swollen by the Police War Reserve, established by the government to offset the depleting effects of conscription on Met strength. Some 20,000 men wore sworn in as Police Reservists between 1939 and 1945.

Women on the march

At the start of the First World War another sizeable workforce was making its mark in munitions factories and other manual jobs, which for centuries had been the preserve of working-class males. Women were quite literally 'on the march' and within a few years they would be patrolling London's streets.

Between 1905 and 1914 the Suffragette movement's campaign of petty vandalism and civil disobedience aimed at securing votes for women had, for the first time, brought the police into direct conflict with ordinary women. But Mrs Pankhurst's followers had a profound effect on the Metropolitan Police in two ways. First, when the Suffragettes suspended their campaign at the outbreak of the war and redirected their energies to filling the gaps in the labour force, many enrolled in the institutions that were the foundation blocks of the Women Police. Second, the minor public-order problems caused by the militants highlighted the limitations of having an all-male police force. The sight of big, burly policemen forcibly

arresting normally law-abiding women on the streets was an unedifying spectacle and played into the Suffragettes' hands. What better publicity could the campaigners have gained to denounce the male 'establishment's' oppression of women?

The activities of the various women's patrol groups organised by the National Union of Women Workers (NUWW) from 1914 onwards gave an inkling of how the Met could benefit from a more diverse labour force. The concept of women police officers had been touted previously but few people took it seriously. A facetious article in the magazine *Modern Society* in 1896 poked fun at the idea. 'Fancy getting "run in" by a sweet little dimpled lavender-scented miss with an 18-inch waist and a dear little retrousé nose! Imagine such a one, attired in a poult-de-soie navy-blue tunic and the latest thing in Parisian helmets, delicately waving a jewelled truncheon and telling us to move on! Oh rapture!'

Early attempts to introduce women officers were undermined by their narrow role, which was more akin to guarding the population's morals than police work. Many of the patrols organised by the NUWW attempted to prevent prostitution in areas around military bases or

Above An early picture of the Metropolitan Women Police Patrols led by Superintendent Sophia Stanley (front left). Recruits had to be unmarried or widowed, and between 25 and 35 years of age.

monitored the behaviour of alleged 'immoral women' who were not prostitutes and had committed no criminal offence. But a Home Office Committee set up under the chairmanship of Sir John Baird in 1920 made a series of recommendations on the employment of women in the police service. It concluded: 'we are of the opinion that in highly populated areas, where offences against the laws relating to women and children are not infrequent, there is not only scope, but urgent need for the employment of policewomen'. The Baird Committee recommended that women should be given limited powers of arrest and improved pay.

The Met had acquired its first full-time policewomen two years earlier. In 1918, Met Commissioner Sir Nevil Macready approved the establishment of the Metropolitan Women Police Patrols under the command of Superintendent Sofia Stanley who was awarded Warrant Number 1. Mrs Stanley's recruits had to be unmarried or widows and between the ages of 25 and 35. They were given uniforms and sent out to patrol areas that were frequented by prostitutes, but they had no power of arrest and were given a distinctly lukewarm reception by many of their male colleagues. Even Commissioner Macready, who had given the green light to the Met's first experiment with female officers, made it clear that, as far as women were concerned, there were limits to his largesse. Giving evidence to the Baird Committee, he stated quite clearly that he did not want 'vinegary spinsters' or 'blighted middle aged fanatics' joining his force. The Met, like other constabularies, later managed to ignore most of the committee's recommendations on giving women officers more status.

In 1931 a Police Federation conference debated the prospect of women detectives. The relevant committee expressed horror at the prospect that wives, sisters and daughters would join the CID while men would be restricted to being 'mere uniform beat sloggers'. Even more unbearable in the Federation's eyes was the possibility that some women would be promoted to detective inspectors 'and order us about so that being on duty will be just like being at home'. Clearly such views were prevalent in many areas of British life at the time and not restricted to the police service.

Progress on equal opportunities in the Met has evolved at a gradual pace, not least because for a sizeable proportion of the organisation's history there were no equal opportunities for women officers. The discrimination was unashamedly institutional. It was ingrained in the Met's structures and procedures in a way that was far more highly developed than the inequalities suffered by other minorities such as black officers. Up until 1946, for example, women had to resign from the force if they decided to get married and were officially barred from any specialist postings such as the CID. Until 1973, women officers were treated as a completely separate service with lower rates of pay than male officers. With each new advance towards equality, complaints that women lacked physical size and strength, or that they were not sufficiently tough or 'streetwise' for police work, were regularly aired by male colleagues of all ranks.

Joan Lock, who served with the Met between 1954 and 1960 and is author of *The British Policewoman: Her Story*, puts the debate about size into perspective. She says that during her time of service women were regularly deployed on public order duties, the smaller women being particularly popular with crowds who could see over their heads. 'At five feet four inches, I did not have the buttressing power of a five foot eight man, but we did have several strapping six-foot girls and quite a few weedy, minimum height men.'

After 1973, women were given exactly the same training and equipment as male officers and were not barred from any types of duty. In theory, at least, they were able to compete on equal terms with their male colleagues for promotion.

Deputy Assistant Commissioner Carole Howlett, one of the most senior female officers in the Met today, joined the police just after the women's branch of the service had been fully integrated. 'Evolution has been slow but steady,' she says. 'We are not yet 30 years from

Left Women's uniforms changed with the fashion of the day, as illustrated by this 1968–1973 version, but equal opportunities were slow in coming.

the Sex Discrimination Act [enacted in 1975] and some things take a working lifetime to change. At one stage in order to be a dog handler you had to be able to pick up your dog and throw it over a hedge. The grips on handguns used by firearms units were too big for the average woman's hand. Silly things like that have now been dispensed with.'

Racial equality

Equality and diversity are now built into the institutional fabric of the Metropolitan Police. However, it has been a long and painful process, not least for a few individual officers who have endured the stigma of being 'a first' within the close-knit organisation.

Norwell Roberts, Britain's first black police officer, joined the Met in 1967 and was in the same intake at Hendon Police College as Paul Condon, who went on to serve as Commissioner between 1993 and 2001. PC Roberts, who had been a laboratory technician, freely admits that for young black men in 1967 joining the police 'just wasn't the thing to do'. But nothing prepared him for the overt racism from colleagues he experienced as a young constable during his first posting to Bow Street Station. It was so acute that he often used to return to his section house in tears after a shift. His car was scratched and his notebooks ripped up while a minority of officers at the station told PC Roberts to his face that he was not welcome. 'As a black officer in the station I was totally isolated and I know for a fact that other officers were threatened into not talking to me,' PC Roberts says of his experience. His colour and the police uniform made him stand out in the bustling West End but PC Roberts found much of the public curiosity a welcome diversion from his tormentors back at the station.

The market traders in Covent Garden barracked him, but in a good-natured way, and he became friendly with many of them. 'I took it all in good humour because

one of the things I found in the Service is that you have to be able to laugh at yourself,' he says. Part of PC Roberts's beat took in the South African Embassy at a time when apartheid was at its height. He could not object to duty outside the buildings where he was in full view of bewildered anti-apartheid demonstrators.

Showing tremendous single-mindedness to pursue his chosen career, PC Roberts was eventually posted to the CID where he quickly found he was accepted as part of the team. He went on to win an outstanding commendation for his role in the arrest of five contract killers in 1985 and two commendations for undercover work with the Drugs Squad. He retired as a detective sergeant in 1997, having completed his full 30 years' service in the Met, and was presented with the Queen's Police Medal (QPM) for outstanding service at Buckingham Palace in 1996.

Roberts's long career mirrors the progress that has been made in the Met on the recruitment and retention of black officers. While racism within the ranks has undoubtedly been a problem, positive steps have been taken to ensure that ethnic minority officers are accepted into the Service and develop successful careers. In 1994 the Black Police Association (BPA) was founded to act as a support group for African, Afro-Caribbean and Asian officers. The BPA gave evidence to the Macpherson inquiry into the Stephen Lawrence murder investigation (see chapter three) and provides a forum for minority ethnic employees to air their concerns.

Today the Met has some 2,000 ethnic minority officers. Tarique Ghaffur became the highest-ranking ethnic minority police officer in the United Kingdom in 2001, having achieved the rank of Met Assistant Commissioner. He is currently in charge of the Met's Specialist Crime Directorate.

Protest and disorder

For centuries London has been the focal point of

Above Norwell Roberts, Britain's first black police officer, at Hendon Training School in 1967. He is pictured with fellow recruit Paul Condon (second left) who had become Met Commissioner by the time Norwell retired from the service in 1997.

political radicalism and protest in Britain. This has presented unique policing problems and has regularly cast the Met, in the eyes of its critics, as enforcers of political will rather than keepers of the peace.

From the outset popular newspapers such as *The Times* had argued that a professional, full-time police force was 'an engine invented by despotism'. But any objective historical analysis of the Service's role in maintaining public order would arrive at the conclusion that its interventions have been infinitely preferable to the alternatives adopted in many other western European countries. The term 'riot police', often used in newspaper headlines, is somewhat misleading. Until the 1980s there were no specialist policing units trained specifically for the purpose of crowd control. Even since then, they have been used sparingly and as a small proportion of the total policing contingent.

Another important historical perspective is that the Metropolitan Police was created partly out of genuine public concern that military intervention in events involving large crowds would lead to more social disorder, loss of life and destruction of property.

The anti-Catholic Gordon riots of 1780, which involved five days of disorder and the burning down of Bow Street Police Office and Newgate Prison, were an enduring scar on public life in London. Under the Riot Act, a magistrate could issue a public order for crowds to disperse, after which troops were authorised to open fire in the event of non-compliance. In the Gordon riots, this led to more than 280 people being shot dead by the 10,000 troops who had been ordered in to control the mob.

Since the creation of the Met there have been only a handful of occasions when troops have been called in to control public order. In part, the effects of the political and social upheavals that sparked violent revolution in eighteenth-century Europe were dissipated in London due to the civil nature of the force charged with maintaining order. That is not to say that politicians have not used the Met to achieve objectives that went well beyond the remit of civilian policing. The Coldbath Fields riot in 1833, which saw the first death of a PC on public-order duty, is a case in point. It is significant not only for the death of PC Robert Culley but for the use, with Home Office approval, of

police spies to undermine the activities of groups agitating for social reform.

The National Union of Working Classes was campaigning for electoral reform and a National Convention. Fearing that the movement's republican demands could spark a revolution, the government ordered police spies to infiltrate the group. On learning that the NUWC planned to hold a public meeting in Coldbath Fields, Clerkenwell, the Home Secretary, Lord Melbourne, ordered Commissioners Rowan and Mayne to stop the meeting. The Commissioners argued that they could not impose a curfew – which was effectively what the Whig government was asking for – on the whole of Clerkenwell. A compromise was reached whereby the meeting would be declared illegal once speakers addressed the crowd and banners were displayed. Rowan also stressed to the officers on duty that no violence was to be used except in self-defence. In the mêlée that followed, two officers were stabbed, one fatally, and innocent bystanders got caught up in the fighting as officers moved in to reclaim the area occupied by the demonstrators.

Public anger that the police had been deployed illegally to break up a peaceful meeting was reflected at the inquest into PC Culley's murder. The jury, which returned a verdict of 'justifiable homicide', were treated as heroes. Lack of sympathy for the dead officer was compounded by a Commons Select Committee inquiry into the activities of the police spies who had infiltrated the NUWC. One of the officers involved was sacked on publication of its report. PC Culley left a widow and four children and newspaper reports giving a full account of the 'sad murder of Robert Culley, a policeman' swung public sympathy back in favour of the police. Mrs Culley was later awarded £200 in compensation by the government.

But the memory of the destruction and death during the Gordon riots provoked a different public response to a proposed march by the Chartist movement in 1848. The movement's People's Charter, published in 1838, had set out an agenda to improve the lives of working men but by 1848 a more radical leader, Feargus O'Connor, had championed the use of physical force to achieve their aims. His plan to organise a huge march on Parliament to deliver a petition was thwarted by pre-emptive police action. More than 150,000 special constables were sworn in to police the march, and although the Chartists held a

Far left The Hyde Park riots of 1866 was one of the few occasions in the Met's 175-year history when troops had to be called in to control rioting crowds because police officers were unable to cope.

Near left Met officers pose with striking miners during the South Wales coal dispute in 1910. Although London officers had been ordered in by the Home Secretary, relations with local people remained friendly.

demonstration on Kennington Common the march on Parliament was cancelled.

The Hyde Park riots in 1866 and those in Trafalgar Square 10 years later – which became known as Bloody Sunday – proved too much for the Met and troops had to be called in to restore order. At Hyde Park 28 policemen were crippled for life and Commissioner Sir Richard Mayne suffered a serious head wound, before admitting defeat and calling for army reinforcements. The Bloody Sunday riots, in which Trafalgar Square was subject to a mass occupation by the unemployed, ultimately led to the public humiliation and resignation of Commissioner Sir Charles Warren. The Commissioner had asked the Home Secretary's permission to ban all meetings in the Square, fearing that there would be serious rioting.

His request was granted but he had to deploy 2,000 men around the perimeter of the Square to prevent a mob from storming it. Officers were unable to hold the rioters back and eventually Warren called in two squadrons of Life Guards to restore order. During the fighting that followed, many people were injured and property in and around Trafalgar Square was damaged. The left-wing press argued that the Commissioner had

acted in an unlawful and indiscriminate manner by banning meetings at the Square. When he resigned over a dispute with the Home Office concerning the Jack the Ripper murder investigation, papers that had originally championed the Commissioner as a liberal progressive rejoiced in his demise.

Perhaps the most controversial use of Met officers on public order duties has involved industrial disputes that had nothing to do with London. The system of mutual aid, which allows for smaller forces to be supported by their bigger neighbours, and the fact that the Mutual Aid Coordinating Centre was established at New Scotland Yard has made the Met the focus for national policing operations. During the miners' strike in South Wales in 1910, 800 Met officers were sent to the principality on the orders of Home Secretary Winston Churchill to maintain law and order. The Met reprised this role more than 70 years later during the bitter dispute between Margaret Thatcher's government and the National Union of Mineworkers (NUM) led by Arthur Scargill (see chapter two).

However, the lessons learned from the Met's involvement in South Wales, where relations between locals and London police officers were largely good, stood the force in good stead for the policing of the General Strike in 1926. Hastily arranged football matches between pickets and police and the use of Special Constables instead of regular officers in areas where violence was thought likely to occur, set the tone of the Met's softly, softly approach. Officers played an important role in keeping public transport running but many of the drivers of trams, buses and trains were civilian volunteers so that the police were not seen as 'strike breakers' by the pickets. Although some 60,000 Specials were sworn in for the duration of the dispute, there was little confrontation with the police and when it was all over *The Times* congratulated the Met and started a national fund which raised £250,000 for improving police leisure facilities.

Passive resistance and the peace marches

The same subtle methods have proved equally effective when policing disorder and civil disobedience. By adopting tactics of passive resistance and minimal deployment of crowd-dispersal forces using mounted officers and dogs, the Met perfected the art of controlling rowdy demonstrations. The sight of a single line of officers linking arms to prevent a crowd surging out of control became a familiar one during the Campaign for Nuclear Disarmament (CND) and anti-war protests of the 1950s and 1960s. The occasional helmet would get knocked off and there were a number of violent scuffles, but most of the officers and the demonstrators exercised a level of restraint. The series of protests against the Vietnam War by students outside the American Embassy in Grosvenor Square in 1967 and 1968 were largely uneventful and well controlled. The notable exception was the violent demonstration on March 17, 1968 in which 145 Met officers were injured.

While the police may have been seen as 'Pigs' in the eyes of some of the students, the Vietnam protests in London were in marked contrast to the blazing mayhem in US cities and on the streets of Paris, where the CRS riot police developed a reputation for brutality. On occasion London's police were accused of being heavy-handed but there was no sign of the CS gas or rubber bullets that littered the pavements in other countries. The deployment of the National Guard in American universities, which led to students being shot dead, was a clear indication that London had escaped the worst excesses on both sides.

The 1967/8 Grosvenor Square demonstrations marked the start of more defined police tactics for dealing with public order problems. The A8 department was formed to develop operational orders that could be communicated to everyone on duty at an incident. From then on, officers were formed into units or 'serials' consisting of one inspector, two sergeants and 20 constables. The demonstrations also showed the Met that it needed to put in place mass catering facilities to ensure its officers were fed. The Home Secretary came to visit officers on duty at one of the demonstrations and made the mistake of asking a sergeant if he was being looked after. 'I've had nothing to eat since six this morning,' was the reply.

Blackshirts and bans

The right to demonstrate and hold public meetings is one of the cornerstones of democratic life. But Sir Oswald Mosley's fascist marches through London's East End in the 1930s sorely tested the principle, after which the Met Commissioner was given the power to apply to the Home Secretary for a ban on any event that had a high risk of sparking violent disorder. This power has, however, been used sparingly by the Met.

The issue of banning or imposing severe restrictions on marches and demonstrations is a complex one and commanding officers face difficult decisions (see

Above Mounted police are deployed to break up fighting between anti-fascists and Sir Oswald Moseley's Blackshirts during the Battle of Cable Street, which took place in London's East End on October 4, 1936.

chapter two). Mosley's Black Shirt (British Union of Fascists) march through London's docks on October 4, 1936 – known as the Battle of Cable Street – was stopped not by the police but by anti-fascist demonstrators and local people who erected barricades to halt its progress. Mosley demanded that the police officers escorting his followers clear a path through the barricades and overturned cars to allow his men to continue unimpeded. The officers had a difficult decision to make because the Black Shirt rally was, strictly speaking, legal albeit extremely provocative and liable to lead to disorder. In the fighting that followed, 80 police officers and demonstrators were seriously injured.

Mounted police

One of the features of the fascist marches in London during the 1930s was the regular use of mounted police to control crowds. Since its inception, the Met has used officers on horseback, though the tactic has on occasion been controversial and the use of horses has taken many years to refine. The size and weight of the horses has often proved extremely effective in controlling and dispersing large groups of people, whether or not they are involved in disorder, but the risk of injury is also greater than when using officers on foot.

Probably the most famous use of mounted police was during the first Wembley Cup Final. Billy, 'the White Horse of Wembley' and his rider, PC George Scorey, have become part of footballing folklore. PC Scorey was one of 10 mounted officers on duty at the newly built Wembley Stadium during the 1923 FA Cup final between West Ham United and Bolton Wanderers. Interest in the match at the new arena was intense. The stadium was packed to capacity and around a hundred thousand football fans were locked outside. As King George V arrived to take his seat in the Royal Box the locked-out fans breached the barriers, forcing huge numbers of spectators on to the pitch. PC Scorey used Billy to move the crowd off the playing surface so the players could get on with the game. The action of PC Scorey and his colleagues saved the match and showed how effective mounted officers could be when directing peaceful but disruptive crowds away from potential trouble spots. Mounted officers have been on duty at big football matches in London ever since.

It is a testament to the Metropolitan Police's success in dealing with public order incidents that it was more than a 140 years before a civilian was killed during a demonstration policed by its officers. The Red Lion Square riot on June 15, 1974 was a painful echo of the Battle of Cable Street 50 years earlier. It involved a clash between supporters of the extreme right-wing National Front (NF) party and groups that opposed them, including a loosely affiliated organisation known as the International Marxist Organisation. When police tried to prevent an attack on the NF demonstration, supporters of the left-wing group attacked the police and mounted units were called up to disperse them. Tragically, a

young man, Kevin Gately, died in the mêlée.

The government set up an inquiry into the death under the direction of Lord Scarman who went on to head the inquiry into the causes of the Brixton Riots in 1981 (see chapter two). Lord Scarman's report highlighted the danger of using mounted officers to clear crowds in restricted spaces. The Met learnt a valuable lesson about safe tactics for the use of mounted officers in public order operations. Since the events of Red Lion Square, police horses have never been used to drive back a large crowd without ensuring that there is a wide space into which people can escape.

Rumours of a 'third force'

By the 1960s the sheer number of protests and demonstrations taking place in London was proving to be a considerable drain on police manpower at a time when the Service was not at full strength. The need for mobile groups of officers to deal with spontaneous acts of violence became more pressing. The first such unit was the Special Patrol Group (SPG), which was the prototype of today's Territorial Support Groups (TSGs).

In its day the SPG attracted a level of unwelcome notoriety largely due to the death of Blair Peach, a teacher and member of the Anti-Nazi League, during disturbances following a National Front election meeting in Southall Town Hall in 1979. Mr Peach was found by officers lying seriously injured in the street and later died in hospital. Examination of the teacher's head injuries suggested he had been hit with a truncheon. Although an investigation by the Met identified possible suspects, the Director of Public Prosecutions ruled there was insufficient evidence to

Left Billy, 'the White Horse of Wembley', and his rider, PC George Scorey, have become part of football folklore, for their role in saving the 1923 FA Cup final.

Left An 1895 example of a criminal record card held at Scotland Yard. From 1862 copies of photographs of convicted criminals were held on file by the Met.

proceed with the case. The SPG was immediately put under the spotlight and stories of how it had started to operate as a paramilitary unit became common in the press.

A trade union leader suggested that the SPG was 'developing as a new style of paramilitary force, trained in physical combat and taught how to cause injury'. This was a flight of fancy. The SPG was not a paramilitary force and its officers received no special equipment. It was formed in 1965 as a mobile unit designed to deal with localised outbreaks of crime. Although its original remit was basic crime prevention patrols, it developed other functions such as large-scale searches and public order duties.

The SPG had around 200 officers split into six units, each commanded by an inspector. As a mobile reserve, each unit had a personnel carrier equipped with its own radio channel. Members of the SPG did not receive any specialist training – all of its officers were volunteers drawn from the uniformed ranks. Although all SPG officers were authorised to carry firearms, they did not carry guns routinely when they

were out on patrol. When they went on armed operations they carried standard-issue .38 Smith & Wesson revolvers – not shotguns or rifles. Armed operations involving the SPG were comparatively rare, but the SPG's armed capabilities caught the media's imagination when units were photographed at the scene of the Spaghetti House and Balcombe Street sieges in 1975.

In reality the SPG was not a 'third force' but a flexible, mobile squad of officers that was used to plug the gaps where borough policing could not cope with spontaneous crime and public order problems. The range of incidents it dealt with included the execution of search warrants, searches for missing persons, murder inquiries, football hooliganism, special escort duties and support for anti-terrorist operations. As the organisation of the Met evolved and specialist units were assigned to deal with specific crime problems, the wide-ranging nature of the role was subsumed.The modern-day equivalent of the SPG – Territorial Support Groups – are trained to a higher level than other Met officers in riot control. They are

also used in pre-planned raids and arrest operations where there are concerns that suspects may use violence.

The changing face of crime

Much of the worldwide renown of the Metropolitan Police is founded on its successes in the area of criminal investigation. For many people, 'Scotland Yard' has become synonymous with world-class detective work, while the idea of 'calling in the Yard' became a staple of newspaper headlines and popular crime fiction.

The formation and development of the Detective Branch, as it was known when it was established in 1842, was a direct response to challenges posed by more organised and mobile criminals. With the huge growth in London's population and the elusiveness of travelling offenders, new ways had to be found to identify suspects. The use of fingerprints and the development of other crime-scene techniques and ballistics were a significant part of that steep learning curve.

The Daniel Good case in 1840 is widely seen as the trigger for the establishment of the detective branch, although problems in tracking down wanted criminals had surfaced on numerous occasions before that. Good, who worked as a coachman in Putney, murdered his wife and dismembered her body. After the corpse was found the police were slow to issue a description of Good, who stayed on the run for 10 days before being recognised by an ex-policeman and arrested in Tonbridge. Newspaper reports of the Met's inept attempts to catch Good while he was on the run focused attention on the loss of the small Bow Street Runners detective force, which had been disbanded a year earlier.

Two years later a small detective force of eight officers was set up under the leadership of Inspector Nicholas Pearce, a former Bow Street Runner. The

Detective Branch was renamed the CID (Criminal Investigation Department) in 1878. Howard Vincent became the first Director of Criminal Investigations in charge of 250 men in plain clothes. From 1862 copies of photographs of convicted criminals taken in prison were sent to Scotland Yard – the first known use of 'mug shot' albums to help police and witnesses identify suspects. Vincent played a prominent role in developing the use of this 'Rogues' Gallery' and other forms of criminal intelligence, including the use of the *Police Gazette* to disseminate – 'for police eyes only' – information about crime and criminals throughout the force.

The detectives' lament

However, despite the creation of a dedicated detective force and the development of more scientific methods of identification, public faith in the Met's ability to investigate crime could be fickle and was influenced by sensational newspaper reporting of high-profile cases. 'Stranger' crimes – where the victim appears to be selected at random by their assailant – represented an even greater challenge to Met detectives in the latter part of the 19th century than they do now. The 11 'Whitechapel murders' committed between 1888 and 1891 are classic early examples of how unsuccessful detective work can be ruthlessly exposed to press and public scrutiny.

Left Detectives quickly learnt undercover techniques to help with surveillance operations against target criminals.

An article in *Police Review* in November 1894, entitled 'Why detectives sometimes fail – the difficulties of finding people wanted', represented a heartfelt plea for understanding. In it, a Met detective complained, 'The stupidity of the police and the failure of the detective force are constant topics for the penny-a-liners despite the fact that the British police system has been copied all over the world. The proportion of arrests following crimes is higher in London than in any other city in the world.' In crimes where there were no suspects or clues, the officer asked 'that the public should be more patient with the detective force'. He continued, 'Do not imagine because you hear nothing of a certain crime or other that nothing is being done.'

The early Met detectives quickly learnt undercover techniques to help them with the surveillance of target criminals and to gather evidence. One officer, unable to find a building from which to watch a suspect, used chemicals to darken his skin and posed as an Italian ice-cream seller for two weeks. But it was not long before experienced criminals became surveillance-conscious and aware of the tactics employed by Met detectives. They would grow beards and moustaches to reduce the value of their Rogues' Gallery mug shots and developed other means of slipping through the net. Charles Peace, one of the most notorious armed thieves of the Victorian era, boasted that he could recognise every Met detective on sight and was so confident

about not being caught that he rented lodgings above a police station. A notorious forger of the period escaped detection by lying low for eight months and growing his hair. During that time he learnt to play the cornet and attached himself to a German band before taking his chance to escape across the Channel. The wanted criminal's 'bolt-hole' was two hundred yards away from the house of a Met detective.

The development of identifying fingerprints as a method of recovering evidence from crime scenes and the establishment of a Fingerprint Bureau at Scotland Yard in 1901 by Edward Henry, later appointed Commissioner, was a significant new weapon in the Met detective's armoury. But the game of cat and mouse between London's detectives and its criminals continued. Developments in high-speed communication, motorised transport and the road system were used by both sides to gain advantage. But the old adage that the police rely on the help of the public to detect the majority of crime has never waned. The establishment of new squads and the acquisition of specialist equipment have, more often than not, been in response to new crime problems rather than pre-emptive action.

The capture of Dr Crippen, who murdered his wife and then attempted to flee London under an assumed name with his lover on board a transatlantic passenger liner, owed much to high-speed communications. But this first use of the radio telegraph to alert police about a wanted felon would not have been an issue if the captain of the SS *Montrose* had not read a newspaper report about the murder and become suspicious of two of his passengers.

The Flying Squad's acquisition of two Royal Flying Corps vehicles in 1920 was the first known use of pursuit vehicles by the Met. But the force was not merely saving on boot leather. London thieves were increasingly using fast cars to commit 'smash and grab' robberies and the horse-drawn wagons adopted by the squad on its formation a year earlier had quickly become obsolete. From its earliest days the Squad established a reputation for spectacular crime-fighting, which still stands. This was based on operations in which gangs of criminals were targeted, put under surveillance, ambushed at the scene of attempted robberies and arrested, with the use of force if necessary. It was also the first police unit to be given a 'roaming brief' to tackle serious crime anywhere in London.

Outgunned by anarchists

Attacks by determined criminals have sometimes been so savage in their intensity that the Met has appeared powerless to prevent them. The Tottenham Outrage of 1909 was a single incident involving two armed Latvian anarchists, which led to the death of a PC, a young boy and the wounding of 21 other people. Even by today's standards, the level of violence used and the mayhem caused was severe. Little wonder that it panicked the Edwardian public into asking serious questions about the nature of crime and the Met's ability to respond to it.

Having held a factory wages clerk at gunpoint, the anarchists Paul Hefeld and Jacob Lepidus were involved in a prolonged chase during which they fired more than 400 rounds at their police pursuers – some of whom were armed only with swords and were riding bicycles. PC William Tyler was shot at point-blank range in the face and 10-year-old Ralph Joscelyne was hit and fatally wounded as he attempted to take cover during the shoot-out. At one point during the chase the anarchists hijacked a tram at gunpoint and fired shots at another tram commandeered by police officers. At the end of the chase, Hefeld and Lepidus both shot themselves in the head rather than allow themselves to be captured.

Two years later, Home Secretary Winston Churchill ordered troops to be brought in to assist the Met in an armed siege involving a gang of Latvian burglars who had already shot dead three City of London police officers and wounded three others who had tried to arrest them. The Siege of Sidney Street on January 3, 1911 showed how poorly prepared and equipped the Met was for tackling well-armed and determined assailants.

The gang had gone on the run after shooting five police officers who had attempted to arrest them during a raid on a jeweller's shop in Houndsditch. A national hunt for the gang, including their leader 'Peter the Painter', was heavily reported in the press. This resulted in a tip-off to the police on 2 January, 1911 that two of the gang were hiding in a second-floor flat in Sidney Street in the East End. But despite the time for operational planning that the tip-off gave them, a sizable force of Met officers was pinned down for hours by two gunmen armed with semi-automatic Mauser pistols. Photographs from the scene show Churchill – who had

Above Home Secretary Winston Churchill takes charge of operations during the Siege of Sidney Street in 1911.

Right During the 1940 Blitz 98 Met officers were killed and many more injured. The resulting civil chaos led to a leap in organised crime.

arrived to take operational command of the incident – standing at the corner of Sidney Street surrounded by armed police officers. But the shotguns and rag-bag assortment of other weapons they are carrying were clearly totally unsuitable for an operation of that type.

The Home Secretary was not impressed and immediately after the incident ordered a review of the firearms available to the Met. The semi-automatic Mauser, which had been used so effectively against the police during the battle of Sidney Street, was one of the weapons tested for police use.

The post-war crime wave

The main 20th-century threat to the professional reputation of the Metropolitan Police proved not to be armed crime or the increasing ingenuity of criminals. The spectre of 'volume crime' was looming large. It now seems certain that the 'golden age' of crime reduction that followed the introduction of Peel's New Police will prove to be no more than a prolonged statistical 'blip'. The post-Second World War crime wave marked an astonishing social change. During the 1920s recorded crime in London once again fell below the 20,000 mark, but three years after the Second World War it had risen tenfold to more than 126,000 and by 1959 had reached the 160,000 mark.

The war years were the engine of this statistical explosion in that they organised crime in a way that hadn't happened before. Rationing, the rise of profiteering and the black market opened up whole new markets for dishonesty. Meanwhile, London's depleted policing resources and the Met's role in civil defence and rescue gave professional criminals a unique opportunity to gain a foothold. The special constables and wartime reservists who had been called in to bolster police numbers lacked experience and had other priorities. During the London Blitz of 1940, for example, 98 Met officers were killed in air raids and

more than 500 were injured.

James Morton, a former defence lawyer and author of a number of books on organised crime, says that wartime austerity changed public perceptions about criminality. 'For the first time, respectable middle-class people came into contact with criminals and bought things from them,' he says. Alcohol, cigarettes, petrol, luxury foodstuffs and clothing became a new criminal currency and one that held its value for years after the war ended in 1945. The bombing of London and the civil chaos it caused led to a leap in opportunist crime. By 1944, looting offences had reached an all-time record.

At the end of the war a small group of Flying Squad officers were told to form a Ghost Squad. The undercover unit was to infiltrate the emerging gangs that had grown in size and number on the back of the black market and the West End vice trade that had serviced British and American troops. The squad was led by Detective Chief Superintendent John Gosling until it was disbanded in 1949 due to the Met's chronic manpower shortages. Although it had a brief history, the Ghost Squad left a lasting legacy in that it placed importance on Met detectives' abilities to gather intelligence and recruit informants. Such tactics produced some outstanding results for the Ghost Squad. In less than four years its work led to 769 arrests, the detection of 1,506 cases and the recovery of £253,896 worth of stolen property.

Although many professional criminals managed to avoid the draft during the Second World War, some were inevitably called up and even served in the armed forces with distinction. But once they were demobbed, their military training and familiarity with firearms and explosives could be used for rather different purposes than the army had intended. The growing audacity of London's criminals and their willingness to use violence to achieve their objectives became a

Flying Squad informants helped to secure the early capture of Great Train robber Bruce Reynolds (above) and the rest of the gang in 1963. £47,245 was recovered from a London phone box – a huge amount of money for the time.

major problem for the Met.

During the 1950s the Police Federation argued that the lack of deterrents, specifically the abolition of hanging, had contributed to the rise in violent crime. It also stressed that the death penalty was the only sure protection for unarmed police officers in the face of criminals who routinely carried firearms. The uproar over the hanging of Derek Bentley for his alleged role in the shooting of Met PC Sidney Miles in Croydon in 1952 played a part in the abolition of the death penalty. Bentley, a young man with limited intelligence, was already in police custody on the warehouse rooftop when officers alleged he shouted to Christopher Craig, 'Let him have it, Chris,' before the fatal bullet was fired. The Court of Appeal declared in 1998 that Bentley's conviction had been unsafe.

But the fine legal arguments over the extent of Bentley's culpability in the murder of a police officer could not be applied in the case of the Shepherd's Bush murders in 1966. The shooting in cold blood of three unarmed plainclothes Met officers on August 16 shocked the nation and led to the foundation of the

Police Dependants' Trust to offer financial help to the families of police officers who had been killed. The murders of Detective Constable David Wombwell, Detective Sergeant Christopher Head and PC Geoffrey Fox as they patrolled in their unmarked car focused political attention on the increase in armed crime and led to calls for the return of capital punishment.

The three men who carried out the murders – John Witney, Harry Roberts and John Duddy – were all caught and sentenced to life imprisonment. Witney was traced swiftly because a member of the public took down the registration of the get-away vehicle he was driving. He was released from prison in 1992. Duddy was traced to Glasgow and died in jail. Roberts, an ex-soldier who had seen active service in Malaya, hid out in the woods for 90 days before being captured. He is still in prison and has expressed no remorse for shooting the officers.

The new villains
By the time of the Shepherd's Bush murders a new underworld 'pecking order' had established itself in London. Gangland figures such as Billy Hill, the Kray

Twins and the Richardson brothers used violence to extort money and acquire nightclubs and other businesses as fronts for their illegal activities, which included sophisticated frauds. Their reputation for violence made it difficult for CID officers to get people to give evidence against the gangs. Detective Chief Superintendent Leonard 'Nipper' Read eventually resorted to using a secret task force working outside New Scotland Yard to gather evidence against the Krays and persuade witnesses to come forward to end their reign of terror and murder.

This type of pro-active, intelligence-led police work became more of a feature of the Met's approach to tackling serious crime. In 1960, C11 branch was established at New Scotland Yard to compile and analyse intelligence about major criminals. This type of intelligence proved invaluable in tracking down those responsible for the Great Train Robbery in 1963, one of the most audacious crimes ever committed. Although the robbery occurred outside the Met's area in Buckinghamshire, the early realisation that London criminals were responsible for the robbery meant that Scotland Yard was called in to assist from the outset.

Those responsible for the theft of £2.6 million in cash from the Glasgow-to-London mail train were arrested quickly due to successful enquiries made by Met detectives in the capital. The network of informants developed by the Flying Squad proved crucial. Fingerprints had been found at the Buckinghamshire farm from which the robbers had launched their raid. Back at Scotland Yard, Detective Chief Superintendent Tommy Butler, a highly experienced Flying Squad officer, was able to tell fingerprint branch staff where to look for likely matches. In this way the Train Robbery team was identified in 24 hours instead of the weeks that a routine search would have taken.

The detailed descriptions of the men, who went on to be convicted for the robbery, and their lifestyles is testament to the thoroughness of the intelligence held in the Met's files. Bruce Reynolds, who planned and directed the robbery, was described as 'a smooth talker and has travelled extensively'. He was 'fond of dog tracks and likes fast cars (anything hotted up)'. He may not live in 'expensive surroundings although he spends freely'. Buster Edwards was described as 'well built but inclined to be getting corpulent'. He was also 'inclined to be aggressive and a gambler'.

But the robbery served as a stark warning that the horizons of organised criminals had widened significantly and the Met and other forces needed to 'think big' in response. The establishment of regional crime squads to tackle criminals who did not restrict their activities to any particular area was hastened. Despite the arrests, only £335,000 of the stolen money was recovered. In one extraordinary incident £47,245 was recovered from a London phone box. The realisation that criminals were not only surveillance conscious but had the ability to keep the police themselves under surveillance was a problem that needed to be solved.

A report on the 'lessons learned from the Great Train Robbery', which was co-authored by senior Met officers and other forces involved, makes sobering reading. It urged forces to 'think in a big way and do not hesitate to involve the resources of the police service on the widest scale. This should be done at once regardless of cost'. On the security of police communications the report warned that 'the vulnerability of the police wireless network to monitoring by those engaged in crime renders it essential to direct police action so far as possible by telephone rather than radio. In this and many other large scale crimes there is clear evidence that the culprits were aided considerably by information heard over the wireless network'.

Corruption

The Train Robbery investigation proved that Scotland Yard's CID knew 'the enemy'. But familiarity between Met detectives and London's underworld came at a price, and it was not long before successes such as this were being weighed in the balance by allegations of serious corruption involving the Met's crime-fighting elite.

The reality is that the various investigative squads and units – some of which have become household names – were both experimental and controversial inside and outside the organisation. The 'Dirty Squad' (Obscene Publications), the 'Rubber Heels' (anti-corruption) and the 'firm within a firm' (corrupt association between detectives) are some of the less flattering old-fashioned references to various types of plainclothes police work in the capital. The process of

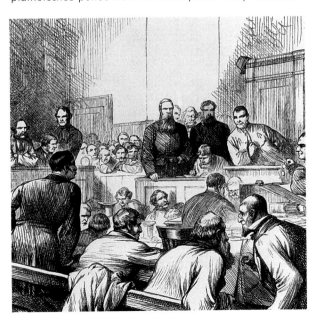

Above Four Scotland Yard detectives stand in the dock at the Old Bailey during their infamous corruption trial in 1877. The scandal led to a government inquiry into detective work.

investigation and the use of informants have at times brought the London police in much closer proximity to professional criminals than Peel's original blueprint had envisaged. While this has proved essential for the detection of serious crime, it has also exposed officers to the risk of corruption.

The 'Trial of the Detectives' in 1877 precipitated one of several shake-ups designed to root out the bad wood. The trial centred on a fraud case in which a rich French woman, Madame de Goncourt, was duped out of £30,000 in a horseracing scam. The confidence tricksters were arrested and convicted but made allegations about their associations with several London detectives. One, Inspector John Meiklejohn, had been in the pay of one of the corrupt bookmakers for several years and had been tipping him off about police enquiries into his activities. In all, four officers stood trial on corruption charges and three were convicted. The trial created a huge public scandal, which precipitated a Committee of Inquiry and the creation of Howard Vincent's new CID.

One hundred years later another prominent Scotland Yard detective stood in an Old Bailey dock facing charges that would cause an even bigger shock wave. On July 7, 1977 a judge sentenced former Flying Squad commander Ken Drury to eight years in prison after a jury found him guilty of five counts of corruption. Five years earlier an article in a tabloid newspaper had alleged that Commander Drury had been on a luxury holiday to Cyprus as the guest of a well-known Soho pornographer, Jimmy Humphreys.

In that year Sir Robert Mark became Commissioner and set out to eliminate institutionalised corruption in the CID. He called a meeting of the various branch representatives and gave them a stark warning. 'I told them that they represented what had long been the most routinely corrupt organisation in London, that nothing and no one would prevent me from putting an end to it and that, if necessary, I would put the whole of the CID back in uniform and make a fresh start.' During the anti-corruption inquiry that followed, more than 70 officers from the Obscene Publications Squad and Flying Squad were investigated, including three senior officers. Thirteen were charged and faced trial while eight were sacked and 40 left the Met on early retirement. It was later alleged that the 'Dirty Squad' had received £250,000 a year in bribes in return for turning a blind eye to the activities of West End vice barons.

DAC Gilbert Kelland, who had been ordered by Sir Robert Mark to conduct the inquiry, later observed, 'Such a scandal involving so many senior detectives… had not occurred since the notorious Trial of the Detectives case in 1877. The Met and its friends were shocked and saddened by the news. The only satisfaction that I and my small investigating team had was that we strongly believed, for the eventual benefit of the force, the crow of corruption had to be publicly nailed to the barn door.'

Special Branch

Contrary to popular belief, there was no single defining moment when the Metropolitan Police Special Branch (MPSB) can be said to have been created. It was a gradual process that occurred over a number of years during the 1880s. The process commenced early in 1880, when events in Ireland and the United States made it obvious that a new phase of activity by extreme Irish nationalists was imminent. Chief Inspector John Littlechild of the Scotland Yard-based Criminal Investigation Division (CID), formally designated as Section A, was instructed to make himself acquainted with all matters to do with Ireland.

The first bomb exploded against the wall of Salford Barracks, Manchester on January 13, 1881. The perpetrators were an Irish-American group known as the Skirmishers and they continued to carry out attacks,

including two in London on March 15, 1883. Within four days of these attacks, a new intake of CID officers, to be known as Section B and consisting of two inspectors, two sergeants and eight PCs, had been placed at Littlechild's disposal. Over the coming months, the Skirmishers were put out of action but were replaced by a more sophisticated threat from the larger, better-resourced group from the USA known as Clan na Gael. Increasingly sophisticated home-made bombs continued to explode, including one left in an outside urinal attached to the wall of the office used by Special Branch at Scotland Yard itself. Damage was extensive and records were destroyed but fortunately no one was seriously injured.

The objective of the bombers was to force the British government to leave Ireland, but the bombers themselves, their explosives and money all came from the USA, not Ireland. Specifically to counter this, Section C was established and 56 Metropolitan Police officers were permanently stationed at every port where passengers from Ireland or the USA disembarked. They were also sent to Europe and operated from ports in France, Denmark and Sweden.

The final addition to the Central CID structure took place in early 1887 with the formation of Section D. It was this small unit of officers, tasked with monitoring extreme Irish nationalists, anarchists and nihilists, that by November 1887 was producing reports on paper headed 'Home Office Crime Department – Special Branch'.

The IRA

Extreme Irish nationalism had brought Special Branch into being and it was the need to combat it that had the greatest long-term impact on Special Branch as an

Right The bomb attack against Scotland Yard by extreme Irish nationalists in 1884 caused extensive damage and destroyed records. The device had been attached to a urinal outside the office used by Special Branch.

organisation. The Easter Rising in Dublin during April 1916 lit a smouldering fuse that burst into flame in 1919 when the IRA began a widespread and violent campaign in Ireland to expel the British administration and establish Ireland as a nation state. Special Branch worked closely with the Royal Irish Constabulary (RIC) and 'G' Branch of the Dublin Metropolitan Police (DMP). While most of the violence was confined to Ireland, by the autumn of 1920 IRA attacks were occurring regularly on the British mainland. In the most serious incident in London, shots were fired at police officers and up to 20 men attempted to set fire to an

oil storage depot in Wandsworth. The declaration of the Irish Free State in 1921 saw an end to the majority of the attacks but serious incidents still occurred, such as the murder in 1923 of Field Marshall Sir Henry Wilson on the steps of his home in Belgravia.

By the early 1970s, the situation in Northern Ireland had deteriorated into violence and terrorism and on March 8, 1972 the Provisional IRA signalled its intention to attack targets outside Northern Ireland. It subsequently left car bombs in London, outside the Old Bailey, an army recruiting office in Great Scotland Yard, the British Forces Broadcasting Office and at New Scotland Yard itself. The

Above A Met officer helps a barrister injured in a Provisional IRA car bomb left outside the Old Bailey in 1973. On the same day the terrorists carried out several other bombings.

bomb outside New Scotland Yard was discovered because of the alertness of two Special Patrol Group officers at the site, and was subsequently safely defused.

An alert went out to all Special Branch officers at ports to find and detain any potential culprit who might be trying to return to Ireland. With the assistance of airline staff, Special Branch officers at Heathrow identified and arrested 10 suspects, all of whom were later convicted. Meanwhile, a frantic search was under way to find and defuse the remaining three car bombs. All were located and evacuations were proceeding when the car bombs exploded.

The battle against the IRA on the mainland would extend over the next 20 years, a period when they carried out over 620 bombing and shooting attacks. Special Branch was to play a key role in both preventing many terrorist crimes and in the long, complex post-incident investigations that brought many members of the IRA to justice.

Public order

Almost from its inception in 1829 as a uniformed, preventative police force, the Metropolitan Police began to deploy officers in plain clothes to gather intelligence on groups that were considered a potential threat to public order by disturbing the peace or inciting others to do so. By the end of the 1880s, Special Branch officers regularly attended meetings held by those involved in seeking 'Home Rule for Ireland', anarchists, social revolutionaries and émigré groups of numerous nationalities. The primary objective was to ensure that no breach of the peace occurred and to gather intelligence as to their current and proposed activities. The period after the Russian Revolution of 1917 saw an upsurge of groups sympathetic to the aims of Communism and Trotskyism and by the 1930s there was also an active extreme right-wing movement, mainly focused on the British Union of Fascists (BUF), led by Sir Oswald Mosley.

The 1970s and 1980s were unprecedented in the breadth of the public order challenge that faced the Metropolitan Police, and Special Branch intelligence played a major role in informing the operational planning and keeping ground commanders in touch with events as they happened. Groups from the extreme left and extreme right sought to cause disorder at marches, demonstrations and protests. Their presence on the streets under their own name often sparked opposition, as at Lewisham in 1977 when a march by the National Front (NF) led to violent disorder and attacks on the police officers escorting it.

The 1990s was to see a gradual decline in the number and frequency of demonstrations connected to domestic events and an increase in those that had an international flavour. Special Branch provided their uniformed colleagues with intelligence and information on the groups involved, the political situation that had led to the demonstration in the first place and whether other attending groups were supportive of the demonstration, or intent on opposing it.

Special Branch today

The threat from international terrorism is not a new one. The early 1970s saw a growing involvement of Special Branch with countering the threat posed by extremist groups linked to the turbulent politics of the Middle East and, later, Armenia, Kashmir and the Punjab. However, the events in the USA on September 11, 2001 showed that mass casualty attacks by groups capable of operating on a global scale had now become a reality. Special Branch continues to fulfil its vital role in protecting the public as part of the wider UK counter-terrorism structure and, uniquely among police institutions, it has been able to reinforce links with the Special Branches of other countries, as well as being able to forge new relationships in countries that do not have a past rooted in a common model of policing.

As the largest Special Branch in the UK, the MPSB carries out a range of activities. Their role at ports was established in the 1880s and today officers are permanently stationed at Heathrow and London City airports and Waterloo International rail terminus. Here they have a dual function – identifying and gathering intelligence on those who may be involved in terrorism or other forms of extremism, as well as contributing to the overall police effort against serious and organised crime. Nationally, Special Branches are a key 'border agency' and hence work closely with other organisations that have different but complementary functions. These include the UK Immigration Service, HM Customs and Excise, the Home Office and the Department of Transport.

A final function of Special Branch is the provision of armed personal protection of prominent individuals who may be at risk from potential terrorist or other type of attack. The origins of this lie, once more, in the 1880s. Today, MPSB provides highly trained armed officers for the protection of UK nationals in this category and those at a similar level of risk who are visiting the UK from abroad.

The Special Branch has had a long and distinguished history, characterised by a willingness to adapt as necessary to changing threats to the people of London. Today that threat has never been greater and there is no doubt that Special Branch will continue to be at the forefront of countering it.

2 Keeping the peace

Every year there are between three and four thousand public order events that have to be policed by the Met. They vary greatly in size and nature – from spontaneous demonstrations and planned marches to open-air concerts, ceremonial occasions and pageants and events in London's many public parks. All require careful police planning but place different demands on the Service's resources. Some events can be policed with a sergeant and six constables, others will require several thousand officers.

Over the last 30 years the Met has developed a highly professional strategy to deal with these demands. It has always tried to maintain a balance between the public's democratic right to protest and the legal requirement to maintain order, while at the same time minimising disruption to Londoners.

It is important to remember that at the time of the inner-city riots of the early 1980s, the police service was not prepared, tactically or mentally, for the levels of violence that took place. Officers, like the public and politicians, were shocked by what they encountered. However, the training and equipment that have been developed since then have been designed to minimise risk and improve police and public safety.

Left Officers struggle to hold back Beatles fans outside Buckingham Palace as the group received their MBEs in 1965. Techniques involving passive resistance were developed to avoid confrontation.

The dustbin lid riot

There is a photograph of the Notting Hill Carnival riots in 1976 which explains in a single moment the revolution in riot-control tactics and equipment that were rapidly developed by the Metropolitan Police over a period of five or six years. In the picture, officers wearing normal patrol uniforms and standard-issue helmets are running towards a mob. Most of the officers in the picture have their truncheons drawn but they are also holding dustbin lids, plastic milk crates and traffic cones to protect themselves from the hail of missiles being thrown at them.

Tony Speed, who was on duty during the carnival as a uniformed inspector, is visible in the middle of the police charge. He is not holding anything except his radio. 'The only tactic we could think of was to run at the crowd,' he says now. 'I am gripping my radio because the important thing for me was to tell Control, through the chaos, what was happening. You can see a crowd of onlookers in the background and if you look closely there are police officers standing around doing the same thing. People just didn't have a clue what to do.'

There were a large number of injuries to officers during the riot. More than half of the PCs on Tony Speed's serial were injured and some hospitalised with serious lacerations caused by flying glass. 'We had not faced bricks and bottles being thrown at us on the streets of London before,' he says. 'There had just been a bit of pushing and shoving. So we just grabbed what we could and all the residents of Notting Hill lost their dustbin lids.'

After what happened in Notting Hill, the Met learned a powerful lesson about the demands of modern public order policing. From the inception of the Metropolitan Police, officers had been trained to work alone, with the minimum of protective equipment, and to use their own discretion to make decisions. The outbreaks of civil disorder that were to scar London and other cities during the late 1970s and 1980s required a completely different approach.

Large numbers of officers needed to be trained and equipped to act in a way that owed more to military tactics than Peel's idea of a civilian service. Thought had to be given to establishing clear lines of command and to providing logistical support for the 'army of officers' who would be called in to tackle specific incidents. This meant better communications, transport and even catering facilities. Tony Speed went on to help develop the strategy and equipment used by the Met today. He retired from the Service as an Assistant Commissioner in 1999.

The first shields

The first priority for the Met was to develop proper shields that would prevent officers having to resort to dustbin lids. A unit of the Special Patrol Group was taken to a sports field in North London to test the new equipment and develop tactics for its use. The engineering department produced some wooden bottles and SPG officers designated as 'rioters' hurled them at colleagues who were holding the new Perspex long shields.

The SPG sports field experiment was makeshift in the extreme but was a rough prototype of the 'Riot City' public order simulation centres that were later developed at Hounslow, west London and then Gravesend in Kent. The purpose of these centres was to create film-set-style locations with buildings, streets and cars so that officers could be given public order training in the most realistic environment possible.

The Met's first public order training centre was at Feltham and consisted of two hangars in which officers could practise the new tactics and equipment being developed. Long batons were introduced for shield-carrying serials because officers discovered that standard truncheons were useless if officers were holding shields as well. Shin-pads and gloves to protect the lower legs and hands from missiles and petrol

Above Officers armed with traffic cones, dustbin lids and plastic milk crates, charge a rioting mob during the 1976 Notting Hill Carnival. The incident proved to be a milestone for the Service, highlighting the fact that the police were not trained or equipped to deal with large scale disorder.

bombs were also tested. The tactics developed at Feltham went on to be deployed at the Lewisham riots sparked by a National Front demonstration in 1977 – the first in which plastic shields were used by police – and the Grunwick strike the same year.

However, while the men and equipment were now in place, sophisticated knowledge of how they could be used in an effective way was still lacking. It would take the Brixton riots of a few years later to expose flaws in the system.

Lessons from Brixton

The Brixton riots during 1981 were, by some measure, the worst mass civil disorder the Metropolitan Police had encountered since it was established 140 years earlier. The damage to property amounted to nearly £5 million. Twenty buildings were destroyed and 34 vehicles – including four police vehicles – were burnt out. More than 400 police officers and 48 civilians were injured, and nearly 800 crimes were reported during that time.

Despite the toll of injury and destruction, the

disturbances had some positive outcomes for the Metropolitan Police. They focused attention on the need to recruit more ethnic minority officers and led to the setting up of Police Consultative Committees (known today as Police Community Consultative Groups) with community leaders. Better police tactics for containing and dealing with disorder also evolved. Collectively, these developments have substantially reduced incidents of civil disorder and have resulted in community involvement with operational policing that would have been unimaginable in 1981 (see chapter three).

The Brixton rioting was triggered by a plainclothes operation – known as SWAMP – designed to tackle street crime following a big increase in robberies in the area. The stop-and-search tactics used were greeted with hostility but the two flash points to the rioting would, in normal circumstances, have been viewed as routine. One was the questioning of a black youth who had been stabbed and the other was the search of a cab and driver who had been seen by a local officer putting something into his sock (it later turned out to be money collected from fares).

Police numbers were not a problem at Brixton. There were van-loads of reserves parked outside Brixton police station while down on Railton Road – where most of the violence was focused – officers were fighting for their lives. Due to poor communication, senior officers didn't know enough about the situation on the ground to deploy the extra officers.

In the public inquiry that followed, Lord Scarman criticised the tactics used in SWAMP and the breakdown in communications between the police and the black community (see chapter three). Scarman also found fault with the Met's ability to deal with the riots once they had started and said the police had a responsibility to train and equip themselves better to deal with disorder. It is important to note, however, that the Scarman report also made it clear that there were social factors behind the riots over which the Met had no control. High levels of unemployment among young

black men, inner-city deprivation and wider forms of discrimination against the black community had contributed to the frustrations that had spilled over into violent confrontation with the forces of law and order.

Today, the Scarman report is viewed as one of the most valuable catalysts in taking the Met forward both in terms of community policing and the development of public order tactics. The issue of proper protective equipment and the crucial need for a more effective chain of command can be traced back to Scarman's observations and recommendations. After the report was published, the Met conducted another review of public order tactics, headed by DAC Bob Hunt, which established the gold, silver, bronze command structure that has been used in all Met public order operations since.

Below Rioters pelt police with missiles during the 1981 Brixton Riots. The disturbances were some of the worst mass civil disorder faced by the Met in 140 years.

A new department within the Hendon Training School – D15 – was formed to concentrate solely on public order training. Its first task was to hold community disorder courses for all Met officers of the rank of chief inspector and above, and train them in the gold, silver, bronze system of command. This command structure, still used today, created a strategic commander (gold), a tactical commander (silver) and a number of other ground commanders (bronze).

The system cut down drastically on the number of senior officers needed at an incident and gave them a clear idea of the roles they were expected to perform. So, for example, the gold commander would be based at the Special Operations Room, silver would act as the forward ground commander, relaying what was happening at the incident back to the control room, and bronze commanders would be in charge of particular geographical areas or units such as mounted officers.

The importance of planning public order operations and briefing all the officers involved became a major focus in senior officers' training. Operation orders, which would detail the roles and responsibilities of everyone involved in an operation, were now issued as a matter of routine.

The unthinkable 'third force'

After Brixton, questions were asked about whether a civilian police service was equipped to deal with the scale of mob disorder that had been witnessed in south London. Wouldn't a paramilitary unit – a 'third force' between the police and the army, similar to the French CRS riot squad – be the best way forward?

Tony Speed, the official link between the inquiry team and the Met, says that the judge killed the argument stone dead. 'For me the Scarman report was the biggest argument against the so-called "third force" because Scarman was all about preventing disorder and deploying methods like community policing in order to avoid it. It is not until that fails that you need to deploy public order staff and they should come from the same body of people doing the community-based work.'

The new public order machine developed before and after the Brixton riots has stood the Metropolitan Police in very good stead ever since. It is not just a method of riot control but a way of deploying large numbers of police on the ground in any scenario. It allows the Met to deploy uniformed aid across London quickly and provide transport, communications, and command and control, as well as catering facilities. It has been used during the mainland bombing campaign conducted by the Provisional IRA (PIRA) during the past 30 years and is one of the cornerstones of the massive police operation to counter the threat of an attack in London by international terrorists.

Demonstrations, riots, public or ceremonial events and major incidents all place similar demands on the Met; when necessary the special operations room, known as GT (see chapter six), is opened up and the

service is mobilised. GT gets its name from its radio call sign, M2GT. Located at New Scotland Yard, it is the nerve centre for communications and control used during major public order operations. Today, banks of television screens linked to police cameras and CCTV systems all over London give the gold commander a bird's eye view of an operation as it unfolds.

Riot City

After Brixton, the new D15 public order training department at Hendon and the A8 branch became jointly responsible for developing public order equipment. Thousands of officers needed to be trained to use the new equipment and tactics and the 'Riot City' training centre at Hounslow was opened, with an overflow facility based at Greenwich. The community disorder courses for senior officers (chief inspector and above) lasted three days. So many people needed to be trained that the courses at Hounslow were running back to back and sometimes overlapping. No senior officer in the Met was exempt – Special Branch, CID officers and other specialists all did the course so that everyone had an understanding of public order tactics. Computer-aided exercises were developed so that the senior officers could take turns being the decision-maker in a simulated riot. With a map in front of them the senior ranks would have to respond to incidents as they happened and deploy the officers they had available.

On the equipment front, fire-retardant overalls were tested and introduced, with long batons and protective 'NATO' helmets. This innovation was way ahead of its time. Years later, when the police service came under the Health and Safety at Work Act, risk assessments would have to be carried out for every police role. If officers were asked to do something dangerous, which public order duty certainly is, the equipment and training had to be put in place to mitigate the danger.

Jumping the gun

Other more controversial equipment was also tested at Hownslow, although none of it has had to be used by the Met in a public order incident to date. Baton rounds have been available to gold commanders since the Brixton riots and Met officers went to Northern Ireland to see how the RUC had been using them to disperse violent disorder.

Rules of engagement were negotiated with the Home Office about when and where baton guns could be used and a training programme was put in place at Hounslow. A senior officer of commander rank would be given the job at any future riot to take sole responsibility for a 'continuous assessment' on whether baton guns could be used. Final authority would rest with the Commissioner. The original rules of engagement were that the police could only fire baton guns to protect life – the same as for police use of firearms. It was not until much later that the rules were changed so that baton guns could be used for the protection of property, albeit with very strict guidelines when used for this purpose. This was significant because to protect police officers' safety in a riot situation, the gold commander could withdraw his or her serials from the scene of the riot and leave the mob to get on with it. If they did that, however, destruction and looting might follow.

CS gas canisters were also available to Met officers

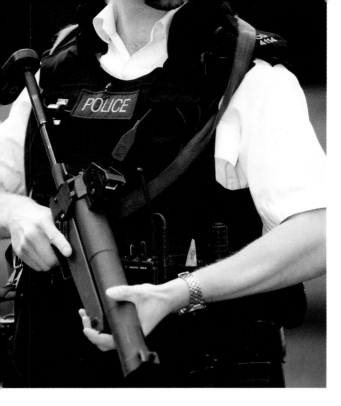

Far left Officers at the Gravesend public order training centre in Kent test their tactics and equipment against a petrol bomb attack. The training is kept as realistic as possible to prepare officers for the highly unpredictable nature of mass disorder.

Near left The Met has trained with baton guns since the Brixton riots, but they have yet to be used in a public order incident.

after Brixton, but officers on the community disorder course were taught that it was unlikely to be used. CS gas is useful for saving life in a hostage situation – in an enclosed space of a building it can be used to confuse and incapacitate the hostage-taker if police have to move in. In the open-air environment of a riot, however, its effects are indiscriminate, so all police officers would need to be equipped with masks. The baton gun teams, who would have fired the CS canisters into the crowd had they been used, were trained in its use at Hounslow. It was often shown to senior officers on the course so that they could see the limitations of CS gas as a tactic.

Many experiments were also conducted at Riot City with water cannon. Tenders used by the West German police were shipped over for testing but the Met public order trainers were unimpressed with them. The tenders quickly ran out of water and had to be refilled constantly. The water cannon option was quickly discarded.

The tragedy of Broadwater Farm

The Tottenham riots of 1985 on the Broadwater Farm estate were the only public disturbances during the 20th century that resulted in the death of a police officer. It was a hugely emotive incident, not just for the police officers who were on duty there and lost a colleague – PC Keith Blakelock – but for local people as well.

After the riots there were genuine attempts at reconciliation. As a symbol of the better relations subsequently reached between the police and the community, there is now a memorial garden on the estate dedicated to PC Blakelock and Cynthia Jarrett, who died from a heart attack during a police search of her home after her son had been arrested and detained at Tottenham police station. Her death was the key factor in triggering the rioting. Whatever the wider causes of the riot, the Met learnt valuable lessons about the importance of early resolution in a disturbance on that scale. Broadwater Farm is a sprawling complex and the challenge of moving large number of officers around the estate in the dark once the trouble had started proved to be a difficult one. Initially most of the rioting was focused on one side of the estate and the main concentration of police numbers were deployed to deal with it. A fire broke out in Tangmere House, which was on the other side of the estate. Black smoke coming from the building indicated that the blaze was too dangerous to leave unattended and officers were required to protect the fire brigade while they attempted to put it out. Word got to the rioters that the police were coming into the back of the estate, and they ran through the walkways to pursue the officers. PC Blakelock tripped and fell and was stabbed to death despite the efforts of his colleagues to drive his attackers back.

Police lines took a dreadful pounding during the riots, though not just with petrol bombs, bricks and other debris. Holes in officers' shields examined afterwards proved that firearms had also been used by the rioters. The violence at Broadwater Farm dissipated as it began to rain and news of PC Blakelock's death spread throughout the estate. This meant that members of the Met's Tactical Firearms Unit were therefore not forced to use baton rounds, the use of which had been authorised by the then Commissioner, Sir Kenneth Newman.

Mounted Branch

Senior Met commanders are trained to have the nerve and confidence to develop strategies, make split-second decisions and choose from a range of tactics to prevent the escalation of disorder, regardless of any criticism they may later face about 'heavy-handed' policing. They appreciate that the right to protest is an important part of democratic life. But legitimate protest can sometimes spill over into violence and when that happens public order commanders have to meet the challenge effectively.

A good example of this was during the large student demonstration at Westminster Bridge in 1992 against the increase in higher-education fees. Violent demonstrators attacked the chief superintendent who was in charge, and then ran on to Westminster Bridge. Police managed to get a cordon across and hold them there. The cordon held for about two hours but the demonstrators were rocking the police coach, which was being used as part of the cordon. Commanders on the ground were worried that if the coach went over, the demonstrators would get into Parliament. As darkness fell, officers in the cordon were getting tired, and as the demonstrators became more violent, police officers started to sustain injuries. Fearing that the situation was escalating out of control, the silver

commander ordered the vehicles and police officers on the ground to withdraw and called in Mounted Branch to disperse the mob. After the demonstration the Met was investigated by an outside force for the way its horses had been used, but its action was exonerated.

Mounted Branch was also used during the printers' dispute outside Rupert Murdoch's News International precinct in Wapping in 1986. During the year-long demonstration, the sacked Fleet Street printers were often joined on their nightly demonstrations by groups such as the Socialist Workers' Party and Revolutionary Communist Party who quickly became known as 'rent-a-mob'. By its 11th month the dispute had taken up almost one million police man-hours. More than 1,200 arrests were made and 362 police officers injured. During one night in May – the anniversary of the start of the dispute – missiles and scaffolding poles were used against police lines, resulting in 170 casualties. Horses were ordered in to disperse the crowd and unfortunately demonstrators caught up in the mêlée were injured.

The Wapping dispute and the miners' strike of 1984–5 were caused by circumstances that the Met had no control over, yet much of the hatred and anger of the protesters was directed at police lines. During the Wapping dispute there is no doubt that groups who had nothing to do with the print industry but were

intent on violent confrontation with the police had attached themselves to a legitimate demonstration by workers who had lost their jobs. This 'rent-a-mob' element was to become a familiar sight for officers at protests in London over the following two decades.

Containment or dispersal?

In a violent public order incident, the gold commander's strategy is based on early resolution, containment or dispersal. If a containment strategy is being used, time becomes a factor. With protective equipment and sheer weight of numbers, police officers could, in theory, contain a violent crowd almost indefinitely. But at some stage order has to be restored, particularly if the containment strategy is resulting in increasing numbers of officers being injured by missiles.

Another public order tactic that can appear to onlookers as aggressive is the use of so-called 'snatch squad' tactics. This involves a group of officers running into a crowd, isolating individuals who are being particularly violent and pulling them out to arrest them. The tactic allows police to continue with the containment strategy while removing the ringleaders. 'Snatch-squads' have, however, been used sparingly in recent years to protect the safety of officers.

One alternative to containment is dispersal, but the Poll Tax riots in 1990 highlighted the dangers of that

Far and near left Masked rioters at Broadwater Farm, Tottenham in 1985. Police lines were subjected to a dreadful battering from petrol bombs, bricks and other debris, and officers were also shot at with firearms. The Met learnt valuable lessons about the importance of early resolution of large disturbances.

tactic. On March 31, 1990 more than 25,000 people marched in protest over the new local tax imposed by the Thatcher government – popularly known as the Poll Tax. The protesters marched from Kennington Park to Trafalgar Square and the route passed along Whitehall and the entrance to Downing Street. Although there was largely what senior officers later described as a 'carnival atmosphere' among many of the protesters, a section of the crowd proved difficult to control. It was clear to officers on duty that this faction had been drinking for most of what had been an unusually hot afternoon in late March. They appeared reluctant to follow the approved route for the march and started knocking over the route markers.

As the protesters went past Downing Street, a significant proportion stopped to gather there, causing congestion and holding up those who were following on behind. As Whitehall became blocked, those at the rear of the protest were redirected by police around the area so that they could gather for the rally in Trafalgar Square as planned. A section of the crowd that had gathered in Whitehall became increasingly violent and started throwing missiles at the cordon of uniformed officers who were guarding Downing Street. Senior officers then decided to try and separate the crowd in Whitehall, using officers in ordinary uniform to push them towards Trafalgar Square at one end and towards Parliament Square at the other. The officers met with resistance and came under attack near the entrance to Trafalgar Square. As the fighting spread to the Square and officers were starting to sustain injuries, police in riot gear were moved in to support their beleaguered colleagues.

As the disorder worsened, mounted officers were used to disperse the violent factions from the Square. This tactic was successful, but rioting continued sporadically for the rest of the evening in other parts of the West End. A section of the rioters who had been driven from the square rampaged through Haymarket, smashing and looting shops and restaurants and overturning cars. During the day some 1,800 crimes were reported, including more than 500 serious offences. The Met arrested 408 people and 542 police officers were injured. The cost of the damage to property was £9 million.

Since the Poll Tax riots the Met has at times chosen to use containment tactics, notably in dealing with public order issues at the annual May Day protests. Professor A. J. Waddington, an expert in the study of public order policing, classes containment as a 'low level of force option', which minimises the risk of fighting and therefore injuries to police and demonstrators. 'It's simple geometry,' he says. 'If you have got a circle of officers around an area, you can contain a volume of people very effectively. The only people who can fight are at the periphery of the circle.'

Renew and review

It has now been 25 years since the Brixton riots, and the strategies developed by the Met to deal with public order challenges have been passed down through each generation of command. Police officers are better trained and equipped and the number of injuries to

officers during public order incidents have been minimised. But the status of equipment and training is constantly being reassessed. For example, following serious disorder outside Millwall Football Club in 2002, which resulted in multiple injuries to officers wearing full riot gear, new kit was issued to better protect the arms, shoulders and thighs.

Today the Met has public order specialist officers who can, when required, support borough colleagues on planned and spontaneous operations, although the decision to deploy officers in riot gear is never taken lightly. While every Met officer is trained in the basics of public order, around 3,000 officers – 10 per cent of the Met's strength – are trained to a higher level. An additional 1,000 officers are trained to an even higher level and they make up the Territorial Support Group (TSG). TSG officers are used regularly on operations of all sizes because of their specialist public order skills.

Carnival and pageantry

The Notting Hill Carnival is, by some way, the biggest policing event the Met deals with on a regular basis. This unique and vibrant festival retains its position as Europe's premier outdoors arts and cultural event and attracts nearly one million people over the three-day August Bank Holiday weekend.

Despite 40 years of experience of policing the Carnival, it remains a challenge for the Met. With huge numbers of carnival-goers gathered in narrow roads, and large vehicles moving through them, public safety

Far left An isolated officer is attacked by demonstrators during the Poll Tax riots in 1990. Although the rioters were eventually dispersed from Trafalgar Square by mounted officers, violence and looting spread to other parts of the West End.

Near left The annual Notting Hill Carnival continues to provide a big policing challenge. Large crowds and narrow roads mean that public safety is the Met's number one priority.

is the number-one priority. A dedicated team of officers at New Scotland Yard works on virtually nothing else but the planning of the event for the whole year.

Around 10,000 officers from the Met, British Transport Police and police staff were used to police the Carnival in 2003. All leave is cancelled for the August holiday well in advance and the operation draws together officers from across London, working under one command structure. The aspiration is that the Carnival should be able to operate and manage itself with minimum intervention from police except in their law and order enforcement role. The policing of the event costs the Met millions of pounds every year.

An excellent partnership between the Carnival organisers, the council for Kensington and Chelsea, Westminster City Council and the Met sees public safety at the top of everyone's agenda. Closer planning has resulted in a more structured stewarding team on the streets of Notting Hill for the event. This means that while the policing operation still involves thousands of officers, they are better supported and can turn their attention to opportunist criminals who take advantage of the crowds. Commander Mick Messinger says, 'The success over the last five years has been based on the relationship between the organisers and other agencies. There is a real energy to make it happen in a safe and celebratory way. And that is after all what Carnival is supposed to be about – a celebration of culture, art and music.' This better co-operation among the partners spans a number of

issues, from the time that sound systems shut down to ensuring that food and drink vendors are licensed. Prompt shutdown remains vital, as the Met knows that if the event runs over the agreed time, it has a knock-on effect – more people on the streets in the early hours of the morning can mean more victims of crime and more arrests.

The September 11 attacks in the United States have changed the face of public order policing, bringing a greater focus on all aspects of security and the potential threat from international terrorism. Any large event such as the Notting Hill Carnival, which is predictable and very well attended, requires a visible and effective policing presence, not only to reassure those taking part but also to act as a deterrent.

Like the Carnival, the vast majority of events handled by the Met are peaceful affairs that require the minimum of police intervention. Ceremonial events, such as Trooping the Colour and other royal occasions, require careful police planning and the co-ordination of many different specialist units, but are largely incident-free.

In terms of officer numbers alone, the state funerals of the Princess of Wales and the Queen Mother were huge undertakings for the Met. A million mourners gathered for the funeral of Diana, Princess of Wales, on September 6, 1997 and many hundreds camped overnight on the streets of central London to make sure they were present as the cortège passed. The event attracted a global television audience estimated at two billion. The policing operation spanned several key sites over several days, and officers had to quickly update plans as the route for the funeral cortège was extended to three times its original length because of the number of people expected to be in attendance. Due to the sudden nature of Diana's death, the entire policing operation had to be planned at very short notice.

Although policing plans for the Queen Mother's funeral in April 2003 were made well in advance of her death, the huge number of people who came to pay their respects over the period leading up to the funeral posed a major challenge. Preparation for policing of the funeral procession and service – Operation Tay Bridge – had been many years in the making, but numerous last-minute changes were needed due to the huge crowds. The involvement of Specialist Operations in the planning was also vital, with the Al-Qaeda attacks in the United States having occurred only six months before. While there was no specific threat level to the event, the policing resources reflected the national and international dimension of the occasion.

Up to 3,500 officers were on duty on the day of the funeral but many thousands more were deployed over the 10 days of state mourning prior to the service. This required massive co-ordination, including a huge catering operation during rehearsals and on the day of the funeral. The Special Operations Room at New Scotland Yard, used to direct policing during major operations, stayed open from the time of the Queen Mother's death until the arrival of the funeral cortège at St George's Chapel in Windsor Castle.

During the weekend when the Queen Mother was lying in state, Met officers monitored the growing queues outside Westminster Hall. The crowd reached more than 7,000 on the Sunday, with queues stretching as far back as Lambeth Bridge. The public, waiting for hours late at night and early in the morning, were cheered when officers handed out cups of steaming tea and coffee. It is estimated that over the four days nearly 400,000 people came to pay their respects. During 12-hour shifts, Met officers were deployed to different areas of the hall: four officers were posted on security duty while those remaining ensured the public continued to file past the catafalque as smoothly and quickly as possible. A public help line based at New Scotland Yard received more than 20,000 calls enquiring about the length of the queue. Commissioner Sir John Stevens said afterwards, 'I was moved by the number of people who took the opportunity to tell me how highly they respected the contribution our police officers had made to this historic occasion'.

While state events can be planned well in advance, one of the keys to success in policing other events like marches and demonstrations is close liaison between the Met and the organisers. Because London is governed by various organisations and authorities, getting permission to hold marches, demonstrations and other public events can be a complex affair, which does not merely mean contacting the Met to arrange proper policing. For instance, if a protest group wishes to have a rally in Hyde Park, it will have to get permission from the Royal Parks Agency; for a demonstration in Trafalgar Square, the organisers will need to contact the Greater London Authority.

The Met's public order planning team has good relationships with all the authorising agencies. They also have long-standing working relationships with all the local authorities, particularly the City of Westminster where the majority of such events are held. Nevertheless, negotiations with protest groups can be tough, given the range of activities and locations their events plan to feature. There are also legislative issues. If the march takes place when Parliament is sitting, Sessional Orders require the

Above Buckingham Palace illuminated during the Queen's Golden Jubilee celebrations in 2003. Even celebratory events such as this demand meticulous planning by the police, and are a major drain on resources.

Commissioner to keep access to the Palace of Westminster completely open so that MPs and ministers can get on with the business of government. That means large numbers of people cannot be allowed to gather outside Downing Street or the House of Commons.

With up to 4,000 events a year taking place in London which require a policing presence, it is inevitable that some events overlap. To ease the burden on London's infrastructure and for the safety of all demonstrators, the Met will assist the organisers in suggesting other areas of London where events could possibly be held. 'It is not our function to assist the organisers to find other places, but in the spirit of openness we will help because there is the organisational expertise at New Scotland Yard,' says Commander Messinger.

Bans and conditions

The Commissioner does have the power, with the Home Secretary's consent, to make an order prohibiting the holding of marches or processions, but only in cases where the Met fears there would be serious public disorder that could not be controlled, serious damage to property or disruption to the life of the community. This power has been used elsewhere in the UK to ban events organised by extreme right-wing groups such as the National Front and its modern equivalent, the British National Party (BNP). The Met has not banned a march since the 1970s, but it has used powers within the Public Order Act to place conditions on marches and assemblies. These powers allow the Met to prescribe a route to groups or set out how long a demonstration can last and where it can take place.

When an Anti-Nazi League march against the British National Party was being organised in Welling in 1993, the route was prescribed by the Met to ensure the safety of both sides. The Met's tactic was to stop the march from going past the BNP headquarters, a bookshop situated in an area of narrow streets in south London. The Met was not acting simply to protect the BNP headquarters – it would have been impossible to allow any type of march to pass through Welling as fire engines and ambulances would not have been able to get through had they been required. A police barricade forced marchers to take a sharp left turn off the road leading to the bookshop. Unfortunately certain sections of the crowd turned their anger towards the police on duty and 19 officers and 41 demonstrators were injured.

Welling was a good example of a comparatively small event presenting many policing challenges because of the explosive issues that were the focus of the protest and the involvement of rival groups. But far larger demonstrations, with similar emotive themes, have passed off perfectly peacefully due to excellent partnerships between the various stakeholders and carefully planned policing.

The Stop the War Coalition's campaign of protest against the government's military action in Iraq saw the main focus of their demonstration take place on the streets of London, although there were other protests all over the UK. Their campaign was supported by other organisations, such as the Muslim Association of Great Britain and CND. Several huge marches were put together involving hundreds of thousands of people. The Met admits that it was surprised by the sheer number of people who turned out for the Stop the War protests, but from a policing perspective this posed no problems. 'The organisation was very good and the organisers were very co-operative. The number of police officers needed was small, relatively speaking, given the huge numbers of people taking part,' said Mick Messinger.

The policing operation for the State visit of US President George W. Bush, in November 2003,

took two months to plan, but in the event passed off peacefully due to close co-operation between the Met, protest organisations and US security officials. The president's itinerary wasn't able to be confirmed until the event itself, which made planning for it even more of a difficulty.

The Met was responsible for the entire operation, from the security of the Royal family and other dignitaries to policing numerous anti-war demonstrations, including the 'Stop Bush' march of November 28, organised by the Stop the War Coalition. A vast amount of planning and liaison were necessary and virtually every specialist unit in the Met was involved. Well over 100,000 demonstrators took part in the march and approximately 5,000 officers were deployed during Bush's four-day visit to the capital.

The outcome of other big events, such as the May Day protests, have been much harder to predict. 'The rationale of May Day is about the onset of summer, celebration, enjoying yourself and being a bit outrageous,' says Mick Messinger.' The numbers that come to the event are hugely unpredictable. There isn't an organiser, and I suspect that is a conscious decision, so it is very difficult to cater for.

Below People gather to protest against the State visit of US president George W. Bush in November 2003. The policing operation took two months to plan.

On the other hand, you can have an event like the Countryside Alliance march in September 2002 where 400,000 people split into two separate marches and took different routes through the centre of London, eventually converging at Whitehall. Despite the size of the protest and logistics involved, only 1,600 officers were needed as the march was so well stewarded.'

The subtle art of policing protest
The May Day protests in 1999 and 2000 were marred by significant disorder and criminal damage to property and buildings. Given that, and the unpredictable nature of the event, there have occasionally been calls from MPs and newspaper commentators to ban it. The problem for the Met is that even if it wanted to take that action, there is no identifiable organiser to issue a ban against. In addition, officers would end up 'policing the ban', which could be even more difficult to do.

Some protests in London involve groups whose ideologies reject the authority of the state and liberal democracy. They see in any issue the same malign forces and will be very easily provoked. The police can quickly become the target of that anger. What has happened over the period of the successive May Day protests since 2000 is that the Met has effectively separated those who wish to hold lawful and peaceful protest from those who wish to carry out acts of violence and cause disorder. Peaceful, organised marches are escorted along the prescribed routes with minimal police interference.

Disorganised, illegal or potentially violent protests attract larger police numbers and tactics of containment are used to prevent violence flaring and spreading to other areas or protesters. In 2003 there was a march led by the TUC to Trafalgar Square. It was in breach of the Sessional Order and was held on a weekday, but the Met allowed it to happen, which effectively secured the adherence of all of the

moderates. There was a sprinkling of more militant extreme elements in the Euston Road but they were easily contained.

Moderate groups are sometimes very good at dealing with outside militant groups that try and infiltrate their protests. There was a miners' protest in Hyde Park in 1992 that followed a government announcement of more pit closures. The march was co-ordinated by the Met and the representative of the National Union of Mineworkers (NUM). A small contingent of anarchists turned up and unfurled an offensive banner. Three or four burly miners went over to the group and told them to take the banner down and leave the protest. They did so without any need for intervention from the police.

City of sport and culture
The streets of London have attracted many thousands of people taking part in numerous celebrations and events over recent years, all of which the Met has policed. Some three million people saw in the Millennium in central London, over two million gathered to celebrate the Queen's Golden Jubilee in June 2002 and most recently nearly one million people welcomed back the England rugby team in December

Above Met officers escort the bus carrying England's victorious Rugby World Cup winners through the West End in 2003. Nearly one million people turned out to line the streets for the victory parade.

2003 after they won the Rugby World Cup in Australia. These crowds do bring with them a significant policing challenge. The Met deployed over 10,000 police officers to deal with the major problem that three million Millennium revellers posed on London's streets. While crowds of this size are unusual, the Met is out in force on every New Year's Eve to police the thousands that throng into Trafalgar and Parliament Squares to hear midnight striking. With no control over the numbers that can attend, the Met has to be ready to deal with any eventuality, and some 3,000 officers were at work on December 31, 2003 to keep the 75,000 revellers safe.

The Greater London Authority (GLA), together with Visit London, is looking to build on the lights and pyrotechnic display of 2003 with a view to the event growing in future years. The Met is already working closely with the GLA and other partners to make sure future New Year's Eve celebrations are both safe and spectacular. Officers from the Met's Public Order Planning Team have travelled to Edinburgh to talk to local officers about how they police the Hogmanay celebrations. In Edinburgh, crowds are controlled by imposing an upper limit and then issuing free tickets through the local authority for the event. 'Anything that could improve New Year's Eve from a public safety point of view would be welcomed by the Met,' says Deputy Assistant Commissioner Stephen House, responsible for Territorial Policing operations. 'Early planning, with all our partners, is key to making this event happen successfully and being able to deal with the huge crowds it would draw. If you think back to the Millennium, when there were more than three million people in central London, it was very crowded. It's about the equivalent to the population of Birmingham. Imagine the load on the transport infrastructure if the whole of Birmingham left to go home at the same time.'

Nevertheless, the Met is far from being daunted by London's bid to host the Olympic Games in 2012. 'It would be great,' says DAC House. 'Given the diverse nature of London's communities, it would be really nice to have a truly worldwide event held in London. It would be a significant security and policing challenge post-9/11, which changed the world of policing. After that the Olympics will never be the same again from a security point of view. But we are up for it and would play a very full part in making it a big success.'

Over the last 30 years the Met has developed the necessary expertise required to deal with the policing challenges that would be presented by hosting such a large event. London is a major cultural, political and economic centre, which makes it an obvious target for terrorists and others whose aim is to undermine the democratic process. It is also a centre for tourism, pageantry and diverse cultural interests. The Metropolitan Police Service justifiably has the reputation of being world leaders in dealing with a huge spectrum of public order scenarios and this plays a major role in ensuring that London's image as a leading world city remains intact.

3 Community policing and diversity

Two seismic events have profoundly shaped the course of the Metropolitan Police over the last 25 years. The changes that were brought about as a result of Lord Scarman's report into the Brixton riots and the inquiry report into the investigation of Stephen Lawrence's murder have affected every part of the organisation.

Although both inquiries focused attention on the police's treatment of ethnic minorities, they forced the Met to ask some fundamental questions about the way it investigated crime and the realities of policing by consent. It has been a long and painful process but the initiatives that have been launched – particularly the new approach to investigating critical incidents and the use of family liaison officers (FLOs) and independent advisory groups (IAGs) – are ground-breaking and have become renowned around the world.

Left A demonstration against alleged police incompetence during the investigation of a New Year fire in Deptford in 1981 which killed 13 black people. The Met now recognises that such critical incidents require a radically different policing approach.

The Stephen Lawrence Inquiry

Some of the criticisms contained in the Stephen Lawrence Inquiry Report (1999) were a painful echo of the problems raised by Lord Scarman after the Brixton riots 18 years earlier. Insensitive policing and a breakdown of community relations were identified by both inquiries as the basic cause of the 'critical incidents' that followed.

The report by Sir William Macpherson was highly critical of the investigation into black teenager Stephen Lawrence's murder, but his recommendations were far more wide-ranging. Like Lord Scarman, he perceived insufficient numbers of black officers, the use of stop and search and lack of trust between the Met and the black community as major obstacles to effective policing. But he went further, citing specifically the treatment of the Lawrence family during the investigation as proof of institutional racism within the Met. Sir William defined institutional racism as 'the collective failure of an organisation to provide an appropriate and professional service to people because of their colour, culture or ethnic origin'. He said it could be detected in attitudes and behaviour that display 'unwitting prejudice, ignorance, thoughtlessness and racial stereotyping'.

Stephen Lawrence was stabbed to death on April 22, 1993 by a gang of white youths while he was waiting for a bus with his friend Duwayne Brooks in Eltham, south London. In May of that year, two youths were charged with Stephen's murder, but in July the case against them was dropped after the Crown Prosecution Service ruled there was insufficient evidence to continue. Stephen's parents made a formal complaint to the Police Complaints Authority about the way the Met had handled the investigation, and an outside force, Kent Constabulary, was brought in to conduct the inquiry.

In 1995 the Lawrences launched a private prosecution against the main suspects, but the Old Bailey trial in 1996 collapsed after the judge ruled that Duwayne Brooks' identification evidence was not reliable enough to be put before a jury. In 1997, Home Secretary Jack Straw announced a public inquiry into the murder investigation, to be headed by retired High Court judge Sir William Macpherson of Cluny. From the day it opened in March 1998, the inquiry was a highly charged and sometimes explosive affair. On June 29 it had to be suspended for four hours after Nation of Islam protesters stormed the hearing as one of the murder suspects gave evidence. Officers had to use CS spray to break up a fight outside. Two people were arrested and charged and four people were taken to hospital.

When Sir William published his findings on February 24, 1999, he echoed the conclusions reached by Kent's investigation on the inadequacies of the initial Lawrence murder inquiry. The decision not to arrest the suspects earlier, when there had been limited evidence against them, was described as a serious strategic mistake. He also criticised the actions of officers at the murder scene, their treatment of Duwayne Brooks and the Lawrence family at the hospital and the failure of many officers to recognise the murder as a racially motivated crime. His report made 70 wide-ranging recommendations on police accountability in the investigation of racist incidents, the treatment of victims and witnesses, stop and search, training, and the recruitment and retention of ethnic minority officers.

The Lawrence legacy

The Met had already started the process of reform before the inquiry was over and Sir William published his report. In 1998 a new unit, the Racial and Violent Crime Task Force, was established to re-investigate unsolved cases where community confidence had been lost. The Met was also well on the way to making

Above The memorial plaque for Stephen Lawrence, the black teenager whose murder in 1993 proved to be a watershed for the Met and its relationship with London's black community.

substantial reforms in how it approached and resourced murder inquiries (see chapter four).

The public inquiry had asked the Met some fairly basic questions about the requirements of policing. One of the main issues was how could police officers get informants and witnesses to come forward if the organisation they belonged to did not have the confidence of the community affected by the murder? The Commissioner at that time, Sir Paul Condon, appointed Deputy Assistant Commissioner John Grieve, ex-head of the Anti-Terrorism Branch and one of its most experienced and successful detectives, to put in place structures that would ensure that 'critical incidents' such as Stephen Lawrence's murder would be handled in a way that gave investigating officers the best chance of success.

The Met soon placed a premium on crime scene management and the importance of the first hour of an investigation when precision and decision-making can mean the difference between success and failure. In dealing with vulnerable communities it also became apparent that family liaison had a critical role to play.

Before the Lawrence Inquiry the Met had thought about critical incidents in terms of how they affected the organisation internally. Decisions would be based on the level of resources required, the impact on other

inquiries and whether the case would generate negative publicity for the organisation. That logic was turned on its head. Senior Investigating Officers (SIOs) were now encouraged to view incidents in terms of the impact they had on the communities affected by the crime. A successful outcome in a murder inquiry was not just about detection but about establishing confidence and trust.

The Met built its Family Liason Officer (FLO) course around one developed by Avon and Somerset Police. The Service has since developed the training and role of FLOs to such a high degree that Met family liaison is now regarded as being the best in the world. It currently has 700 fully trained FLOs who are available on a 24-hour basis to work in London, around the UK or abroad. The Met sent a number of FLOs to New York after the 9/11 terrorist attacks to work with the families of British victims. 'The Prime Minister, the UN Secretary General Kofi Annan and the US President said afterwards that the British system of family liaison was absolutely brilliant,' says John Grieve today. Met FLOs were also sent to Iran following the earthquake in 2003 and to Bali after the terrorist bombings.

The role of family liaison officers in a murder investigation used to be the last to be allocated, reflecting the low status attached to the job. This has fundamentally changed. The presence of trained family liaison officers does not stop relatives asking the police difficult questions about the investigation or being openly critical about the way it is being handled. But, taking the Stephen Lawrence case as an example, the things that Stephen's parents were saying about the inquiry would have been heard a lot earlier and acted upon. The families of murder victims have spoken on the Met's courses about their experiences. 'We treat victims' families as experts,' says Commander Andy Baker, head of homicide investigation at the Met. 'They have more knowledge of the victim than anyone and form an integral part of an open-minded investigation. Who else could know more about the victim than their own loved ones?'

Families are also vital sources of information, particularly in minority communities where lines of communication with the police are not always open or straightforward. 'I don't think the wall of silence really exists,' says Baker. 'The truth will come out in the fullness of time. It is our professional endeavour to relentlessly pursue that truth and bring perpetrators to justice.'

Another significant innovation has been the Met's use of independent advisory groups. Although the concept is similar, this is light years ahead of Scarman's idea of police consultative committees. Advisors have a significant input on Met operations and policy development and are consulted at every level of an investigation. Such freedom of access clearly poses some operational risks, but to date there have been no significant breaches of that trust. The Service has advisory groups at central and borough levels that provide support in critical incidents involving vulnerable communities and other groups. These include lesbian, gay, bisexual and transgender people (LGBT), gypsies and travellers, Tamils, young people, victims of sexual offences and victims of gun crime in the black community.

Senior officers working in the Met's Diversity Directorate say that John Grieve has left a legacy that the Service can be proud of. Commander Cressida Dick, who now leads Operation Trident investigations

into gun crime affecting the black community, was John Grieve's successor on the Racial and Violent Crime Task Force, and worked in Peckham when Stephen Lawrence was murdered. At that time she says she recognised the inability to communicate and recognise cultural differences that was criticised during the Stephen Lawrence Inquiry. She worked outside the Met for seven years but transferred back and noticed a big cultural change in the organisation. 'There was less arrogance, more willingness to listen to other people's opinions and admit it when mistakes were being made,' she says. 'On many levels, the Service was more accountable and more open.'

Despite greater levels of openness and accountability, victims of hate crime and vulnerable communities can still be reluctant to come forward and ask the police to help them because of fear of reprisals or having to give evidence. To this end, the Met has launched two initiatives designed to make it easier to make contact with the police.

Community Safety Units (CSUs) have been set up in every borough of London with dedicated staff who tackle hate crimes, including domestic violence, racist and homophobic attacks. They treat each report of a hate crime as a priority and have put in place systems to ensure that victims are treated sensitively and on a confidential basis if necessary. Victims are also given access to other expert help, including that of doctors and victim support organisations, if this is requested by the individual. CSUs operate a 'positive arrest policy', which means that a suspect will be arrested immediately if possible. This policy is designed to give victims immediate respite from the fear of further harm or abuse and give them time to consider their options. If, for example, victims want to talk to someone privately, CSU officers can give them advice or put them in touch with other organisations that can help. This service is completely confidential. Within 24 hours of a crime having been reported to the police, victims are allocated a specially trained officer who will be a contact point for the duration of the investigation. Every effort is made to keep the victim fully up to date with the case. If, for example, the case goes to court and the defendant is bailed, the victim will be informed and offered additional support if necessary.

In 2003 the Met also launched third-party reporting schemes, which allow individuals to report hate crimes without having to visit a police station. Self-reporting packs have been distributed among London's LGBT community so they can fill in a form to report homophobic incidents. Such incidents can be reported anonymously, in which case the police will use the information as intelligence. If victims want to include their personal details, the crime report will be followed up in the usual way.

The borough of Westminster, for example, has introduced a 'tell a friend' self-reporting scheme aimed at Soho's LGBT community. Reporting packs the size of a credit card, which fit into a wallet, have been distributed around pubs and clubs in the area. An assisted reporting scheme has also been launched through Galop, London's LGBT community safety charity. The scheme acts as a buffer between the police and the victim via specially trained reporting centre workers at the charity who record details of hate crimes. As with the self-reporting scheme, crimes can either be reported anonymously or with personal details. Although the scheme is aimed at victims of hate crime, it has also been used to report allegations of child abuse and drug dealing.

Critical incidents re-investigated
From the time it was established, the Racial and Violent Crime Task Force concentrated its energies and resources on the re-investigation of a number of

sensitive and high-profile incidents involving ethnic minority victims and loss of community confidence. The murders of Stephen Lawrence and Michael Menson are cases in point, along with the New Cross fire of 1981 in which 13 black youngsters died. The guiding principle for these fresh inquiries was Macpherson's dictum that 'a racist incident is any incident which is perceived to be racist by the victim or any other person'.

The Michael Menson case is a classic example of how the Met's new approach to murder investigation could bring perpetrators to justice in even the most difficult and sensitive inquiries. The case, originally hampered by police failings, would eventually take the Met's murder team to Northern Cyprus for an unprecedented murder trial there.

Musician Michael Menson was found badly injured in the early hours of January 27, 1997 in Edmonton, north London. He had suffered terrible burns to over 30 per cent of his body and later died in hospital. Initially, the incident wasn't treated as a murder inquiry but it emerged later that Mr Menson had been attacked by three men. In September 1998, an inquest jury returned a verdict of unlawful killing. The Metropolitan Police issued a statement admitting that mistakes had been made during the first 12 hours of the investigation and announced a new inquiry led by the Racial and Violent Crime Task Force. The re-investigation team worked with Michael Menson's family, leading to the arrest and charge of his killers.

At the Old Bailey trial Mario Pereira was found guilty of murder. Co-defendant Charalambous Constantinou was found not guilty of murder but guilty of manslaughter. Detectives also focused on a third man, Ozgay Cevat, who had been identified as the third attacker. He had been arrested by the Cyprus authorities for an unrelated charge of causing grievous bodily harm. Britain has no extradition treaty with

Northern Cyprus and, knowing there was no way of extraditing him, Met detectives entered into negotiations with police in Northern Cyprus to see if there was another way of bringing him back to face trial. The Northern Cyprus authorities sent a high-ranking police officer to Britain, who told the Met there was a local law that allowed the prosecution of offenders who committed their crimes in other countries. After sustained high-level discussions and unusual co-operation between the two countries, Cevat was arrested, tried and jailed by authorities in Northern Cyprus for 14 years for the manslaughter of Michael Menson.

Another significant case that highlights the commitment by the Met to secure the trust and confidence of minority communities has been the re-investigation into the New Cross Fire.

In January 1981, 13 young black people died during a fire that began at a house party in New Cross. The fire started on the ground floor and spread rapidly through the house, trapping many without means of escape and forcing others to flee by jumping from

upstairs windows. Many suffered severe injuries. The case had a monumental impact on police relations with the black community. The victims' families and their supporters were infuriated by what they saw as an inadequate response to what they believed to be a racist firebomb attack and by a sense of 'establishment' lack of interest in the tragedy. This was compounded by the decision to hold an inquest 12 weeks after the fire, long before the police investigation had been completed. Open verdicts were recorded. The families were upset that the events of that night remained unexplained, and for some the theory of a racist motive persisted. Further sadness occurred when in 1983 a survivor of the fire took his own life, widely seen as being the result of having witnessed the fire and his friends' deaths.

In the aftermath of the inquest the families formed the New Cross Fire Parents Committee, chaired by Mr George Francis, to seek a new inquest. Through their dignified and persistent efforts, in 1997 the Met agreed to conduct a re-investigation into the cause of the fire. With the emphasis on securing community

Left A hard-hitting Operation Trident poster appeals for information on gun crime. Senior Met officers say the operation has been successful mainly because of the efforts of community leaders to sell its message.

confidence, the case passed naturally to the Racial and Violent Crime Task Force in October 2000. The Task Force team examined over 16,000 pages of statements and documentary exhibits from over 750 witnesses. New evidence suggested the fire had been deliberately started in an armchair in the downstairs lounge. Armed with this the Met took the rarely used step of applying to the High Court for a new inquest. The application was successful and a new inquest ordered. This took place in 2004 and evidence was heard from 190 witnesses. The coroner again recorded open verdicts. However he went as far as saying that although he believed it probable that the fire was started deliberately with a flame against an armchair, he could not be sure of this on the evidence and therefore could not return verdicts of unlawful killing.

Despite the families' disappointment at the new verdict, an important shift in perception had occurred. The total professionalism and empathy in the new approach taken during the years of re-investigation meant that, in complete contrast to 1981, the families and their supporters had grown confident in the Met

and its intentions. They even praised the re-investigation work and the officers involved.

Meanwhile, the case that precipitated the sea change in the way the police service deals with critical incidents – the murder of Stephen Lawrence in 1993 – has undergone a third investigation. A file was sent to the Crown Prosecution Service (CPS) in 2002 but in May 2004 the CPS decided that there was insufficient evidence to proceed with a prosecution. Unless new evidence comes to light, officers will no longer actively work on the investigation.

Following the CPS's decision, the Met's Deputy Commissioner, Sir Ian Blair, commented, 'We share the frustration of all those touched by Stephen's murder that his murderers have not been brought to justice for this racist crime. However, because of his parents' concerted drive for justice there is no doubt that Stephen's murder has left a legacy of change, from the improved way that murder and serious crime is investigated to the improved service minority communities now have from the police. There is no question that the innovative way that racial crime is now dealt with through the whole criminal justice service is a tribute to those that have supported Stephen's memory through bad times and good. We remain entirely committed to working closely with all our communities to tackle racism in all its criminal forms.'

Operation Trident

While these three cases have a major resonance for the families involved and the wider community, the Met has applied the same investigative rigour to a specific crime problem that affects the black community.

It is a sad fact that a young black man in London is more likely to be shot dead than a young person from any other background. Operation Trident is very much a response by the police to a plea from a particular community for help. Homicides within the black community involving firearms in the late 1990s were increasing at an alarming rate. Trident originated from an operation targeting firearms crime in Lambeth. It was soon adopted across London boroughs, and in July 2000 was established as a policing command following concerns by the Met and the black community that more needed to be done about gun-related incidents affecting black Londoners.

The majority of these shootings were being committed by black criminals on other members of the black community, but the levels of casual violence used and the fear the shootings generated meant that there was a paucity of witnesses and information. Trident's role was to co-ordinate intelligence and resources for officers investigating these gun crimes. Trident now has more than 300 officers divided into dedicated murder investigation teams, an intelligence team and a proactive capability unit. It also has its own independent advisory group. Since 2000 it has achieved some high-profile successes. Between 2002/3 and 2003/4 there was a 50 per cent fall in murders and a 22 per cent reduction in attempted murders. This was undoubtedly the best year yet for Trident.

It is very difficult to provide a specific policing service to a particular community without stigmatising them, particularly when notions of gangsterism and a street culture based on guns and drugs are already associated with the black community by some sections of public opinion. Assistant Commissioner Tarique Ghaffur says Trident has a difficult balancing act to perform but has managed it successfully mainly because members of the black community have put a huge effort into selling the operation's message. It is now very well known and an area of policing that people clearly have confidence in. Cressida Dick, Commander in the Serious Crime Group, says, 'Some people trust Trident a lot more than they trust the Met generally. They see it as their operation – a good thing that the Met has done for them.'

In a wider sense, the black community's admission that it has a problem with gun crime has made the Met's job a bit easier. Lee Jasper, a member of Trident's IAG and police advisor to the Mayor, has written and spoken publicly about the issue, which he has described as the biggest threat to the black community since its arrival in Britain in the 1950s. Commander Dick says that 10 years ago, if the Met had talked about black gun crime, it would have been castigated for being racist. Now the community is openly talking about the issue, particularly in the black press.

Trident still deals exclusively with gun crime in the black community but recently the operational command unit took on the investigation of non-fatal shootings in other communities, known as Operation Trafalgar. One of Trident's major achievements has been giving communities enough trust and confidence in the Met for people to come forward and give evidence against the gunmen who are blighting their lives. Four or five years ago the detection rate for gun crime in the black community was below 25 per cent, compared to more than 70 per cent for all other shootings.

Often the shootings were fast-moving incidents with few witnesses, but those few that were available were extremely reluctant to come forward. Many people who witness a violent attack on the streets would be nervous about giving evidence in court. But if the attack happens within your community, the fear of possible reprisals for co-operating with the police is heightened. Trident has invested very heavily in witness protection schemes to give people the confidence to come forward. 'The operation has led the way in witness protection, not just in London but nationally,' says Detective Chief Superintendent John Coles QPM, who heads up the Trident unit. This doesn't often involve giving people new identities and moving them to another county to prevent the gunmen enacting

Above Lee Jasper, police and race equality advisor to London's Mayor, has described gun crime as the biggest threat to the black community.

their revenge. 'For a lot of people, that is not at all what they need. We are much more imaginative in how we offer them protection and often use independent advisors.'

Trident murders often take a great deal of investigating. Nurturing the confidence of the community to produce intelligence, converting that into evidence and getting individuals to court safely to testify takes an enormous amount of work. One of the Trident teams recently said that on average it takes four officers to persuade witnesses to give evidence on the day of the trial. 'A lot of the witnesses have complicated lives and are fearful of standing up in court and giving evidence.'

A major asset to Trident investigations has proved to be Crimestoppers – the independent national charity started in 1988 to help police gather intelligence, make arrests and solve crimes. Callers who contact the Crimestoppers hotline are guaranteed anonymity and may receive a reward for their information. In 2003, intelligence passed on in this way led to 577 arrests in London – 30 for murder. Almost £1 million in property, drugs and firearms was also recovered.

Trident's independent advisory group gives general advice about how the operation will be perceived by the black communities and they are heavily involved in the creation of publicity material and appeals for information. The poster campaigns, radio and press commercials and award-winning advertorials have become a trade mark of the operation. The Met consults IAG members on virtually every initiative, including high-profile street operations involving armed officers. Members of the IAG have been down to the firearms training centre at Gravesend to see how professionally officers are trained and what the constraints are. Frequently the IAG will go on armed operations with the Met to see the theory put into practice and to talk to any members of the public who may have concerns about the number of armed police in the area. There is a sense that the Met can now conduct intensive anti-crime operations in sensitive areas of London which a few years ago would have caused community unrest. 'We have to prepare the ground, involve the IAG, tell them what the intelligence is telling us, why a particular street is a hotspot for gun crime and what we are trying to achieve,' says John Coles. 'We would then ask them what they think. Ten years ago we would have just hoped for the best, now it is tailored to local issues and local people.' IAG members also advise on specific homicide cases to support the senior investigating officers and the strategic thinking. They are also able to report back to the Met the reaction of the local community to the investigation and if there are any issues with the victim's family that need to be dealt with.

The Met believes that it has made good progress on arresting and convicting some of the most violent and dangerous people. In 2002, one of Operation Trident's most prolific offenders was given a 12-year sentence for kidnap, torture and blackmail. Mark Lambie was described by officers as Trident's

Above A Scenes of Crime Officer examines a firearm recovered from a shooting incident. Many of these weapons are converted firearms that have been reactivated by criminals.

'core nominal' – a ruthless and violent criminal who considered himself above the law. He is believed to have been responsible for a catalogue of offences right across London and his conviction was lauded as not just a landmark case for Trident but a major success for the black community. Lambie, 30, leader of the notorious Tottenham Man Dem Crew, was sentenced, along with three others, for kidnapping and torturing two men with a hammer, an electric iron and boiling water. The offenders believed their victims were involved with drug dealing and had access to large amounts of cash. Lambie terrorised his local community over many years, and his reputation for violence was enhanced by the unusual alliances he made with other gang leaders. Nine of the witnesses in the case, who would more appropriately be described as victims, had to be put under the Met's witness protection programme.

Despite such high-profile convictions and the significant overall reduction in homicides and attempted homicides achieved by Trident operations, there is still a hugely disproportionate impact of gun crime on black people in London. There are also worrying signs that an increasing number of young men are gaining access to firearms and carrying them either as status symbols or for protection. Many of these weapons are converted firearms – weapons that have been sold as deactivated weapons but are then reactivated by criminals. Their accuracy is haphazard to say the least but they are still dangerous.

So where are most of these weapons coming from? The National Criminal Intelligence Service (NCIS), which conducted an assessment of the illegal firearms market, found that some of them are being bought over the internet and others are smuggled in as military hardware from war zones around the world. Some are available to buy legally as so-called imitation firearms – where the firing mechanism has been removed – and

are then illegally machine-tooled so that they can fire live ammunition.

Some of the media and the public mistakenly associate black gun crime with Jamaican gangsters who are involved in violent crime and the drug trade, and travel back and forth to Britain as illegal immigrants. In fact, most of the cases handled by Trident officers involve British-born African-Caribbeans who have no Jamaican connection. About 15 per cent of all Trident murders involve Jamaicans and many are in the UK legally. Where there is a connection with Caribbean-based criminals, London's police can widen the net of the investigation through co-operation with other police forces. Trident officers have worked closely with the Jamaican police to stem the import of crack cocaine into the UK and prevent 'men of violence' coming here.

Another challenge for the Trident teams is that the gun violence they are investigating is extremely hard to predict. Violent incidents can blow up, seemingly out of nowhere, and over issues that appear quite trivial. Trident detectives who have worked with the Flying Squad, for example, are used to dealing with criminals who work in tight-knit teams and use weapons to threaten but rarely open fire. Trident criminals tend to be more chaotic in their use of violence. Friction between two individuals over a matter of 'respect' can either be settled over a cup of coffee or end up as an extremely violent murder. Trident 'nominals' – those individuals who are listed on the Met's database of target criminals – also regularly rob each other of money and drugs, knowing that rarely will the incident be reported to the police.

A change in culture

The MPS has achieved remarkable successes around diversity. Top-level commitment, the allocation of resources and a determination to open up the processes and structures of policing to external scrutiny have changed the organisation. More than 370 critical incidents have now been managed with members of independent advisory groups integrated into the process. Nearly 40,000 Met employees have been through the Community and Race Relations training. The Racial and Violent Crime Task Force, and now the whole of the Met, have demonstrated that investigative strategies that involve communities deliver better results. The culture of the organisation will no longer tolerate racism or bigotry, and language has changed. The MPS is regarded as a world leader in many of its diversity approaches and, while continually learning from constructive challenges presented by partner organisations, is regarded positively for the strategic efforts it has made.

Commander Steve Allen, who now heads the Met's Diversity Directorate, said, 'The MPS has responded with energy, imagination, commitment and professionalism to a crisis. The crisis was Macpherson and the catastrophic failures exposed by that inquiry. The debate about the response is one about sustainability and how far the experience of our communities is different because of the changes. How far have we achieved what we set out to and therefore can we now move on, philosophically and resource-wise, to a new and different challenge? Have we 'done' diversity?

'At the heart of these questions must lie the MPS understanding of what diversity means in a policing context. There is a choice between having "diversity" as a module on a course or as an organising philosophy upon which all our activity is based. Where diversity is seen as a competency rather than as a way of understanding the world, the MPS will fail to deliver appropriate operational service. If the diversity agenda is simply about satisfying demand for policies, initiatives and strategies then the MPS has done its bit. If, however, there is a desire to make a continuing and sustainable change to the street experience of those receiving policing service then the journey is far from over. If we want the organisation to feel different to those of our people who derive from under-represented and minority communities, the road stretches out for miles in front of us. There remain too many occasions when people's experience of the MPS fails to match up to our rhetoric.

'The diversity agenda is about understanding the significance of difference. It is not about tolerating difference or knowing the rules for entering a Gurdwara. The agenda is about knowing that each of us has a particular perspective on the world, driven by upbringing, community history, experience and opportunity. The agenda is about individuals and the organisation opening themselves up to challenge from a whole range of perspectives in order that services are not distorted by bias and ignorance. It is not about how many black people and women we can get to join the Service – it is about creating an organisation that black people, women and everyone else wants to join.'

4 The specialists

The name of New Scotland Yard is recognised throughout the world and the Met's experience and expertise at handling major murder inquiries has, throughout its history, led to requests for assistance from other UK forces and other countries.

But the range and scale of serious crime committed in London - 70 per cent of all organised crime in the UK is based in the capital - has meant that the Met has built up a number of highly specialised police units to tackle not just murder but a range of other crimes, and to provide a national and international lead in their area of policing expertise.

In November 2002 the Service amalgamated all these units within the newly-formed Specialist Crime Directorate (SCD) under the direction of Assistant Commissioner Tarique Ghaffur. The SCD tackles all aspects of serious and specialist crime, including gun crime, organised crime in London's vulnerable communities, Class A drugs offences, economic crime, and cases involving children as the victims of serious crime. The SCD also provides vital back-up services such as forensics, the Service Intelligence Bureau and the Crime Academy.

Murder investigation

To ensure that its standards remain world class, the Metropolitan Police has made a significant investment over the last five years in the training of its detectives and the resources devoted to its murder squads. Under Commissioner Sir John Stevens, the Service has built a new structure for the investigation of murder and other major crimes, which is designed to tackle the problems identified by the public inquiry into the investigation of Stephen Lawrence's killing in 1993.

Under the old AMIP (Area Major Incident Pool) system, teams of CID officers were based at each area headquarters. AMIP detectives were responsible for investigating murders and other major crimes that either crossed divisional boundaries or were thought to be too big for divisional detectives to deal with. The heavy caseload of the Met's murder detectives and the lack of resources under the AMIP system were identified as significant weaknesses by the Stephen Lawrence Inquiry. 'After the Stephen Lawrence Inquiry, the challenge for the Met was to restore our reputation,' says Deputy Assistant Commissioner (DAC) Bill Griffiths, a senior officer with Scotland Yard's Specialist Crimes Directorate, which is responsible for murder investigation. 'We were determined to be a world leader once again.'

Now all the officers with the Major Investigation Teams (MITs) are permanently attached. Under the new system a senior investigating officer (SIO) – usually a detective chief inspector – runs three core teams led by a detective inspector, together with the Major Incident Room (MIR) staff and an intelligence cell. Each MIT will have the core skills needed to run a major inquiry. This will include a disclosure officer (to ensure that the

Left An officer stands on duty outside the home of TV presenter Jill Dando after she was shot dead on her front doorstep in April 1999. The case was one of the most challenging investigations in the Met's history.

right material is given to the defence in the event of a trial), an exhibits officer (who ensures that material evidence is properly collated and kept) and a family liaison officer (to provide a link between the victim's family and the investigating team). Each individual detective will be a specialist in a minimum of two murder investigation skills, and the rotational nature of the system means that officers will get the chance to use all their expertise across a range of investigations. The system is designed to allow each SIO to manage multiple cases effectively. In the Met each SIO will have at least 10 cases on the go at any one time. This workload is far higher than detectives in provincial forces would have to manage and reflects the fact that London is the largest city in the UK.

The investigation of murder in any police force can be divided into three distinct categories:

- A – major crime which causes grave public concern. Examples of this category includes child murder, multiple murder or the murder of a police officer;
- B – major crime where the offender is unknown (e.g. high-profile, complex inquiry);
- C – major crime where the offender is known. Such cases would include domestic murders.

So-called 'stranger murders' represent some of the most challenging cases for detectives. One of the most high-profile 'stranger murder' investigations undertaken by the Met was the one conducted into the murder of TV presenter Jill Dando in 1999.

The murder of Jill Dando

On April 26 Miss Dando was shot dead on the doorstep of her home in Gowan Avenue, Fulham, shortly after leaving her fiancé's home. She was killed by a close-range shot to the side of the head from a 9mm semi-automatic pistol. Witnesses indicated that a man had been spotted hanging around outside the

Above A poster appealing for information in the Jill Dando murder investigation. After six months the investigating team had interviewed more than 2,500 people and taken 1,100 statements.

house prior to the shooting.

The investigation lasted more than a year, and with no apparent motive to go on, detectives were faced with a massive task. Jill Dando was a public figure known to millions. Her status as a television celebrity brought her into contact with a large number of people, any one of whom may have had a connection with the shooting. At one stage in the inquiry detectives had a list of 2,000 persons of interest to them, including many hundreds of fans who had bombarded the presenter with letters. There was also speculation that Jill Dando's work as a 'Crimewatch' presenter may have attracted the attention of London's underworld and that the shooting had been of significance. But there were other possible motives for the shooting which officers also had to consider. Early in the inquiry, for example, it emerged that Miss Dando had received a letter from a 'Serb source', attacking a charity appeal she had made for Kosovan refugees two weeks before her death. There was massive public and media interest in the inquiry. After the first 'Crimewatch' reconstruction, officers received more than 500 calls. After six months, officers on the murder team had spoken to more than 2,500 people and taken some 1,100 statements. Detectives arrested Barry George, also known as Barry Bulsara, following enquiries into his behaviour immediately following the murder and a period of surveillance on his home. They believe he had followed Miss Dando on several occasions before he killed her. His eventual conviction for the crime demonstrated that pieces of circumstantial evidence taken together could, despite common misconceptions, be used to build a strong case. For example, two fragments of forensic evidence linked George to the killing. A tiny spherical particle of firearms residue composed of barium, aluminium and lead was found inside the right-hand pocket of a blue jacket owned by George. Similar discharge residue particles were discovered in Miss Dando's hair and on her coat. They had been deposited when the gun was fired, producing a cloud of chemicals. A fibre from George's trousers was also matched to a similar fibre recovered from Miss Dando's coat.

When George was arrested, he told detectives he had never heard of Miss Dando before her death, and did not know Gowan Avenue, even though the road was less than half a mile from the flat where he had lived for 10 years and his doctor had been in Gowan Avenue, two doors away from Miss Dando's house. Three witnesses had spotted George in Gowan Avenue in the hours before the murder.

George initially denied featuring in a photograph that showed a man wearing a respirator and holding a gun, but changed his story when detectives told him it had

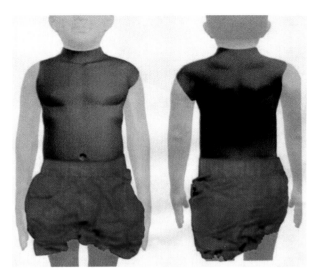

Above The torso of 'Adam', a victim of ritual murder, as shown in a Met reconstruction. The body of the young boy was recovered from the River Thames with the head and limbs removed.

been taken from his home. Detectives found numerous newspapers, handwritten notes and photographs relating to BBC programmes when they searched his flat in Crookham Road, Fulham. There were also four copies of the BBC in-house magazine, *Ariel*, published shortly after the murder, which featured Miss Dando on the front cover. He had numerous other press cuttings on the killing. The jury was not told that George had a criminal record, which had marked him out for police attention long before Miss Dando's murder. When he was 22 he had been convicted at the Old Bailey of attempting to rape a language student. George was convicted for murder at the Old Bailey in July 2001 and received a life sentence.

'Adam' – a ritual killing

One of the most complex investigations that the Met has undertaken in recent years is into the murder of 'Adam', a little boy believed to have been killed as part of a ritual. Despite a unique and exhaustive investigation, the true identity of 'Adam' is yet to be discovered and the investigation remains ongoing.

On Friday, 21 September, 2001, the torso of a young black boy aged between four and seven years was recovered from the River Thames near Tower

Bridge in London. A post-mortem revealed that the child had been killed by a violent trauma to the neck and he had been drained of all his blood. His head and limbs had been skilfully removed and he was dressed in a pair of orange shorts. The pathologist suggested that the child may have been the victim of a ritual murder. The investigation team, led by DI (now DCI) Will O'Reilly, sought the informed view of a South African pathologist; he confirmed his colleague's earlier fears that this was very likely to have been a ritual murder known as a 'muti' murder after the Zulu word for medicine (the reason they are called muti murders is that different body parts are used in the making of various tribal 'medicines').

The first step of any murder investigation is to identify the victim – this could lead to the victim's relationship with the killer(s). Extensive enquiries throughout the UK and beyond into Europe did not produce any leads. The investigation team began to believe that the boy had been born elsewhere and brought to the UK.

Public anxiety was such that, following a review of the case, a chief officer was deputed to oversee the inquiry – Commander Andy Baker, Head of Homicide Investigations for London. The team worked hard to engage the public with £50,000 being offered as a reward for information. Andy Baker declared the Met as the child's family until his rightful family were found. The team was also keen to name the boy to put a stop to descriptions such as 'The Thames Torso'. The name 'Adam' was chosen so as to avoid any obvious link with any region or faith.

The team travelled to South Africa to find out more about ritual murders and to follow up an offer from Nelson Mandela to make a worldwide appeal. The team also visited cultural advisors and one suggested that the child was most likely to have been an offering to a water goddess. Another line of enquiry was to identify the child's country of origin. The team tested the resources of the Met's Forensic Science Service and called on other forensic experts to assist. In time, this extensive team undertook ground-breaking analysis. Mitrochondrial DNA and Y-chromosone comparisons suggested that the child had come from West Africa. Tests on Adam's bone constituents, working on the principle 'you are what you eat', suggested that there were elements of pre-Cambrian rock that covered five countries in West Africa, with the biggest land mass being in Nigeria.

Detective Chief Inspector (DCI) O'Reilly and scientists went to Nigeria and recovered soil, animal and human samples to test against the composition of Adam's bone structure. It was discovered that Adam had come from a narrow corridor between Ibaden and Benin City in south-west Nigeria. Oceanography suggested that the child had been placed in the Thames in the London area, and pollen grains typical of London trees and plants were found in Adam's intestine, confirming that he had been alive – and more than likely killed – in London. Other particles were found inside Adam – most notably pieces of the Calabar bean, a plant indigenous to West Africa, which can cause paralysis without a loss of consciousness and is known to be used in witchcraft.

It is the opinion of the investigation team that Adam was brought to the UK illegally, almost certainly through Europe (the provenance of the shorts identified them as having been bought in Germany or possibly Austria), and that he was specifically brought for the purposes of a ritual murder. Ritual murders are committed for many reasons, although the reason for Adam's is still unknown. The investigation team has undertaken extensive research into the areas of ritual murder and human sacrifice and found the practice of human sacrifice is known throughout sub-Saharan

Above Detective Chief Inspector Will O'Reilly and Commander Andy Baker with Nelson Mandela at a press conference. The 'Adam' investigation team travelled to South Africa where an appeal was launched to try and identify Adam and his killers.

Africa; indeed with the shrinking world and movement of people, it is now found across the world. A strategic working group has since been convened to learn more about these beliefs to identify methods of preventing homicides. The team has been told that their commitment is recognised by many and has prevented other such murders taking place.

The ground-breaking forensic work used in the 'Adam' case has since been used to identify the places of residence of unidentified bodies and is also now being used to trace the familial background (known as familial DNA) and ancestral background of suspects.

The investigation into Adam's murder is ongoing and the Metropolitan Police Service is determined to find out what happened to Adam and bring the perpetrators to justice. The team has smashed a major human trafficking network and papers naming three suspects have been submitted to the Crown Prosecution Service. The officers, police staff, scientists, independent advisors and others who have worked on the case are determined to provide Adam with a dignified burial and

reunite him with his family, who may be unaware that he has met such a terrifying death.

The importance of case reviews

A lesson from the Stephen Lawrence Inquiry is the importance of having a proper system for taking stock and reviewing a murder inquiry, particularly in cases that have stalled and appear to be going nowhere.

The Met now feels it has a murder review system that is second to none. If a case is not solved within 28 days it is subject to a review. This involves a senior detective from outside the inquiry team going through the investigation with a fine-tooth comb. In high-profile cases the review will happen much sooner – perhaps within a matter of days. Far from treading on the toes of the detectives leading the investigation, the fresh pair of eyes is welcomed as part of the inquiry. Detectives always want to know whether anything has been missed or if there is a fresh line of enquiry that needs to be taken. With the Met investigating around 200 murders a year, as well as other critical incidents, having a separate team of senior detectives to review the work of those conducting the actual investigation would be a great drain on resources, so the Met has pioneered a system of using retired senior detectives – currently 28 review officers and 18 research officers – to do most of the review work.

The Met often receives requests for assistance from overseas police forces involved in murder investigations, particularly if the victim is a British citizen. However, the number of requests outweighs the available resources and the Commissioner often has to turn down requests.

The new approach

The lessons learnt from the mistakes surrounding the investigation into Stephen Lawrence's murder were put into effect after the murder of 10-year-old Damilola Taylor in 2000. Damilola was found bleeding to death on a Peckham estate in south London. He was taken to hospital where he died of his injuries. A subsequent post-mortem concluded that he had died from loss of blood caused by a single stab wound to his left leg. Two teenage suspects were acquitted of the murder in 2002 after the testimony of a key witness was discredited by the defence. The case remains open.

At the time of the murder all eyes were focused on how the Met would handle the case, and not just because it involved the killing of someone who was so young and vulnerable. Although other murder investigations involving ethnic minorities had been tackled since the Stephen Lawrence case, the media were looking to make unfavourable comparisons with other high-profile cases.

During the inquiry, to gather information, the Met deployed a team of black officers on the estate where Damilola was killed. 'What that achieved was a better response from the public to our enquiries, and I think the team gave a lot of reassurance to the public as well,' said DAC Griffiths. After the trial Commissioner Sir John Stevens ordered an independent review of the investigation and prosecution of the case to establish what lessons could be learnt for the benefit of future investigations. The oversight panel, chaired by Bishop John Sentamu, concluded: 'Overall, the Metropolitan Police Service response to Damilola Taylor's murder is a manifest example of how the MPS has moved on since its unsatisfactory investigation of the murder of Stephen Lawrence in 1993. The panel believes that it is important that this is acknowledged. The MPS commitment to improving the investigation and detection of offences of murder is illustrated in many aspects of this case. The panel also believes that there are demonstrable differences between the police handling of the investigation of this case and that of Stephen Lawrence – in particular, the commitment and effort of those who responded to the incident and those involved in the investigation, the provision of early and sustained family liaison and the commitment and involvement of senior officers which will enable the MPS and its community stakeholders to work towards developing higher levels of confidence and trust in the ability of the MPS to understand and respond to crimes of major concern.'

Critical incident simulations

The Met has invested heavily in the training of detectives. All Met detectives are now trained using the HYDRA simulator suite at Hendon Training School. HYDRA was developed by Dr Jonathan Crego to train police officers in the strategic and tactical management of both large-scale critical incidents and major crime

investigations such as rape and murder. It allows command officers who would typically be responsible for managing large teams to work together in syndicates on a common problem within a safe training environment. HYDRA has been developed to simulate more protracted incidents and investigations that may take days or weeks to resolve. In the case of major inquiries, the system can simulate an investigation spanning several months.

Students are split into three groups and each one has to manage an ongoing murder investigation, simultaneously working through the exercise from the same starting point. Each officer takes it in turn to be the decision-maker in the inquiry and each action is recorded. After several hours the 'live inquiry' is stopped and all the detectives are assembled to compare notes about how decisions have been taken. During each training exercise a central control room sends a simultaneous stream of information to each of the three syndicate rooms. This could be in the form of video or audio clips, photographs or documents. The idea of the simulation is to replicate the complex flow of information and actions arising from major inquiries. Detectives are immersed in a real unfolding event to give them a feel of what it is like to be involved in such an incident. The control room is staffed by three subject-matter experts who use the system software to respond to each group's call for information.

The simulation is dynamic so that the scenarios presented to each group change constantly in line with the decisions taken by each SIO. During the exercise officers also have to analyse witness statements and forensic evidence against a background of highly volatile family liaison requirements and intense outside scrutiny from the media, chief officers and government ministers. Each incident unfolds in real time and there is a range of possible outcomes that can be thrown at the students by the controller of the exercise. All decisions

are logged so that when the groups are brought together at the end of each session, the actions taken can be discussed among the groups.

Every detective inspector and detective chief inspector in the Met – more than 600 officers – has been trained on the simulator. The majority of these officers are not involved in murder investigations but borough detectives may initially be sent to the scene of a murder, and the first few hours after a murder has been reported are vital to the investigation's success or failure. Securing the scene of the crime, which may cover a wide area, finding witnesses and establishing good family liaison are all vital initial tasks.

Ideally, when a murder occurs on Met territory, divisional CID officers will use those 'golden' first hours to enable the officers that follow to succeed. The homicide assessment team – the 'first wave' from the Specialist Crime Directorate – then arrive to make sure everything is in place for the on-call murder team to take over.

The Crime Academy

The term 'New Scotland Yard detective' is rightfully associated worldwide with policing excellence. But much of this reputation is built on skills and

Far left The Crime Academy equips Met detectives with a wide range of skills including dealing with the media and using press conferences as an investigative tool.

Near left An organisation the size of the Met employs people with a wide range of personal skills and knowledge such as linguists and community experts. The Community and Cultural Resource Unit is able to tap into this expertise.

experience that until recently have not formally been part of training but were simply passed on from detective to detective.

The Met established a Crime Academy in 2003 to capture the knowledge and experience of its best detectives and incorporate that expertise into properly assessed training courses. Based at Hendon Police Training College, the Academy provides a foundation course for investigators and specific courses for the ranks of detective constable and detective sergeant. The training covers initial investigation at the scene of a crime through to presenting evidence in court. Assistant Commissioner Tarique Ghaffur says, 'The Commissioner in particular wanted a renewed emphasis and rejuvenation of investigations and detective skills.'

The academy is launching a foundation degree for detectives so that investigative skills and experience can be recognised by a formal qualification. There are also plans to establish formal links between the Met's Academy and other famous policing academies around the world such as the FBI training school in Quantico, Virginia. The Met's investment in training and resources for those specialist officers who deal with the most protracted and complex crimes appears to be paying

off. In 2003 the Met achieved a 97.5 per cent detection rate on murder.

Community-based initiatives

An important investigative tool that was developed on the back of the Damilola Taylor investigation is the Community and Cultural Resource Unit (CCRU). In an organisation the size of the Metropolitan Police, there are people with a vast range of skills and knowledge – from being able to speak a second language to in-depth understanding of various religions. The CCRU is a resource centre that enables investigators to tap into that expertise.

Volunteers' names are kept on a confidential database and made available to investigating officers and incident commanders. The database is maintained by 12 CCRU co-ordinators of inspector rank or above. The CCRU has provided considerable assistance in a number of sensitive investigations. For example, five Bengali-speaking officers were used to make door-to-door enquiries following the murder of an elderly Indian woman in Whitechapel. There had been tension in the area between police and the Bengali community, which made up 80 per cent of the local population. The Bengali-speaking officers visited the scene of the murder on the night the murder took place, and were able to speak to members of the community and gauge what was being said about the incident. In another imaginative use of CCRU resources a Met officer who can use sign language was drafted in to help an investigation into assaults on three gay deaf men in Soho. The assaults had occurred on a 'deaf night' at a local pub and the officer was able to go back to the pub and communicate with the clientele and appeal for witnesses to come forward. The CCRU has led to a number of community policing initiatives, such as a regular patrol of a predominantly Algerian community in North London by an officer who can speak Arabic.

Above Nail bomber David Copeland captured on CCTV in Brixton, south London. Investigating officers seized a total of 1,097 videotapes containing 26,000 hours of footage in their efforts to identify a suspect.

Another step forward in securing community involvement in sensitive major inquiries has been the role of independent advisory groups (IAGs). IAGs are made up of community advisors who can be actively consulted about police operations. They provide a vital link between the Met and the community so that sensitive inquiries are handled in a way that will not alienate support from that community. The Service has advisory groups at central and borough levels. There are also separate IAGs that provide support in critical incidents involving vulnerable communities and other groups. These include lesbian, gay, bisexual and transgender people, rape victims, Tamils and black victims, particularly of gun crime.

Operation Marathon

Some types of crime, particularly hate crime, can impact beyond the immediate victims and their families. It is vital for the Met to gain the confidence of communities affected by hate crime, not just because it leads to mutual trust and respect but past experience has shown that an increase in trust usually generates more operational intelligence.

An example was the Operation Marathon investigation in 1999, conducted by the Anti-Terrorist Branch, that followed the atrocious crimes committed by nail bomber David Copeland. During his brief reign of terror, Copeland targeted the black community in Brixton, the Asian community in Brick Lane and then the gay community in London's West End. During the course of the three bombings it appeared highly likely that the bomber had a deep hatred of certain minorities and that the campaign of attacks was designed to foster fear and division in London's minority communities. It also became clear that people with no involvement in the bombing used the attacks as an opportunity to spread their messages of hate by making false claims of responsibility.

Left Detectives who arrested Copeland at his home in Farnborough found that his bedroom walls (far left) were covered with Nazi flags and press cuttings about bombings and racist violence.

This was a highly sensitive inquiry and the Met worked hard to give reassurance to the communities who were being targeted with devices that were designed to cause appalling injuries and loss of life. Against this background officers had to work extremely quickly to catch the bomber.

As one attack followed another, and with precious little in terms of initial leads, officers worked against huge odds. A mammoth technical effort was required to sift vast volumes of evidence for a few precious fragments that could lead to the identification of the person or persons responsible. Although it proved impossible to find Copeland before he carried out his third and final bombing, he was caught in a remarkably short space of time and his arrest undoubtedly prevented further attacks.

Copeland's first attack was directed at a busy shopping centre in Brixton, south London on April 17, 1999. Two street traders had noticed a dark holdall at a bus stop. It was still there minutes later so they carried it around the corner and looked inside. They saw what appeared to be a bomb packed with nails.

They moved the holdall away from the stalls. A man then walked up, removed two boxes from the holdall, placed the boxes on nearby wooden pallets and walked away with the bag. Police were alerted. As officers were being spoken to and were approaching the bomb, the explosion occurred, causing horrific injuries. More than 1,590 nails of various sizes were recovered from the scene, most of which were bent and were consistent with having been in close proximity to an explosion.

Police were careful in the immediate wake of the Brixton blast not to rule out any possibility, but it became clear that the bomber obviously had a hatred of certain sections of the community and officers made great efforts to work with all communities that might be targets. The Met instigated immediate and regular meetings with community representatives. There were also regular police briefings to members of London's black, Asian, gay and lesbian communities.

A total of 1,097 CCTV videotapes were seized after the Brixton attack, potentially containing around 26,000 hours of footage. All of this had to be checked

– much of it one frame at a time. There were technical complications in checking the tapes. The majority of them had been recorded using 'multiplex' systems, meaning that each tape held footage from between two and 16 cameras. Each frame on a tape could contain several images – each from a different camera – and in many cases there were problems with image quality.

One stroke of luck was that officers were able to recover, intact, the black bag in which the Brixton bomb had been planted. They were then able to begin searching the video footage for people carrying bags of that type. Police forensic teams searching the scene of the explosion recovered fragments of the alarm clock that had been used as the timer. They were able to identify the brand of clock and officers began checking shops that sold that particular kind of clock and bags of the type used in the Brixton bombing. They found that a large chain of catalogue stores sold both items. When Copeland was later arrested, receipts for clocks and a bag from the chain store were found among his possessions.

Officers examining CCTV footage from Brixton found a pinprick image of a man who was first seen carrying a bag similar to that which contained the bomb and then without the bag. The image was extremely blurred but the Met was able to call in outside technical expertise to enhance it.

Copeland planted his second bomb on Saturday, April 24, in east London's Brick Lane, a thriving business centre for the area's Asian community. A man in Brick Lane noticed a black sports bag, with a well-known sports logo on the side, lying on the ground in front of a parked white transit van. Thinking the bag had been lost, he carried it to a nearby police station, but it was closed. He put the bag in the boot of his car but, remembering the recent bomb in Brixton, he became suspicious and dialled 999 on his mobile phone. It was at this time the bomb went off. A few people who were in the vicinity were injured and there

was damage to vehicles and surrounding buildings. More than 300 nails were recovered from the scene with a total mass of almost 3 kg. When Copeland was questioned following his arrest, it turned out that he had believed there was a busy market in Brick Lane on Saturday. Fortunately he was wrong and he was a day too early.

On April 29 the Met's Anti-Terrorist Branch released images to the media from the CCTV footage recovered from Brixton. As a result of the appeals, over 570 calls were received from members of the public. One call was from a taxi driver who told detectives that he had collected a man fitting the description of the suspect from Waterloo station the previous Saturday. The man had asked to be taken to the Brick Lane area. This was the first indication that the suspect came from Southern England. Officers retrieved large amounts of CCTV footage from cameras at Waterloo and were later able to pick out frames containing the suspect. These indicated that he had travelled by train from the direction of Hampshire.

The day after the taxi driver's phone call, Copeland mounted his third and most devastating attack. On Friday, April 30, a man sitting at the bar in The Admiral Duncan public house in Old Compton Street, Soho, a place frequented by the gay community, noticed a man described as being between 21 and 27 years old, 5 ft 6 in to 5 ft 7 in (1.67m to 1.7 m) tall, with short cropped dark hair. This man is believed to have been David Copeland. He ordered a soft drink, but seemed uneasy and kept looking at his watch. Copeland then asked where the nearest bank was and left minutes before the bomb exploded.

Shortly before the explosion, the assistant manager of The Admiral Duncan was directed by one of the bar staff to a bag that did not appear to belong to anyone in the pub at the time. He examined the outside of the bag and asked customers nearby if it was theirs. They all said 'no'. He became concerned and began to move people away before he went back to the bag. As he was standing over it, the bomb exploded. Three people were killed and scores of others in the pub were injured, many suffering extensive burns. Several of the injured had legs amputated and more than 500 nails were recovered from the scene.

After the attack on The Admiral Duncan pub the Met set up a mobile police station in Soho staffed by gay police officers. They were actively deployed in order that people from the gay community felt more comfortable with approaching the police with information. A vital breakthrough came on the same day the pub was bombed. A man who had worked with Copeland saw images of the Brixton bomb suspect in a newspaper published that day. He called the Met's freephone number and told the police he thought the man pictured in the newspaper was Copeland.

Although there was no way of knowing it at the time, Copeland was already in London in the process of carrying out the Soho bombing. He had stayed at a hotel under an assumed name before checking into a different hotel under a different assumed name to prepare his bomb. Unfortunately police had no information that would have led them to him in the period of approximately an hour that elapsed between the call and the blast.

In the very early hours of Saturday, May 1, a number of Flying Squad officers arrested Copeland at his home address in Farnborough, Hampshire, where he had been renting a bedroom for about three months. When arrested and cautioned he replied, 'They're all down to me. I did them on my own.' When officers went into Copeland's bedroom they found the walls covered with Nazi flags and press cuttings about bombings and racist violence.

On June 30, 2000, following a three-week trial, a jury agreed with the prosecution that although Copeland's thinking was a long way from what might be considered reasonable or normal, he was essentially a cold-blooded murderer who was fully responsible for his actions. He received six life sentences for the murders of three people and for causing the three explosions.

The growth in organised crime

Although gun crime represents a small proportion of the total crime in London, the fear it creates is often disproportionate to the reality and its effect on communities is immense. The problem is being tackled by the Met both proactively and reactively. Examples include Operation Trident, which was set up in 1999 to reduce gun crime in the black community (see Chapter three) and Operation Trafalgar, set up in 2004 to investigate all other non-fatal shootings.

A UK-wide threat assessment by the National Criminal Intelligence Service (NCIS) has estimated that 70 per cent of all organised crime is based in London. The problems caused by the gangs are complex, not least with the arrival of new criminal groups from the Balkans, the Caribbean and Russia.

The new arrivals are competing with established groups which are either home-grown or within naturalised ethnic communities, such as the Turkish gangs in north London who have long been thought to control a major slice of the capital's heroin trade. There is also evidence that some of the groups are now working together – one group using another for enforcement purposes, for example. Organised crime in London now involves new communities finding niches for cash-rich, money laundering activities. Much of this activity is drug related but drug routes are also used for the smuggling of firearms and people.

In response to the threat posed by the criminal use of firearms the Met has augmented its own armed capability in the shape of armed response vehicles (ARVs). These are armed mobile units crewed by officers from the Met's tactical firearms unit, SO19. Working round the clock in shifts, they will get to incidents quickly when criminal use of firearms becomes a threat.

This move towards more armed police on the streets was accelerated by the callous murder of a community police officer in 1993 in Clapham, south London. While attending a routine call at a house in Cato Road, PC Patrick Dunne heard gunfire and went into the street to investigate. He was confronted and shot dead by one of the three men who had just murdered a local man named William Danso. After shooting PC Dunne the men were heard to walk away laughing and firing shots in the air. Three men were arrested in 1993 and charged with offences relating to the murders, but the charges were dropped in 1994 on the advice of the Crown Prosecution Service. An active re-investigation into this double murder remains ongoing. The Met already had ARVs when PC Dunne was killed but after the incident their number was substantially increased. They concentrate their patrols on 'hotspots' for armed crime but also provide peripheral cover.

Many of the squads in the Specialist Crime Directorate work regularly with SO19 firearms units on planned operations. This involves a detailed risk assessment of the threat posed by the armed criminals in question and the combination of excellent planning, surprise and professionalism has ensured that, to date, the Met has always come out on top.

The combination of ARVs, better proactive intelligence about armed criminals and hard-hitting policing by the likes of the Flying Squad effectively prevents the London police from becoming a fully armed service. The arming of Metropolitan police officers is, however, kept under constant review. Commissioner Sir John Stevens says, 'The police service in Britain is able to carry out its duties with the consent of the community. Fundamental to that

consent is the fact that our officers are not routinely armed – despite the dangers they face on an almost daily basis. There are more examples of courage and heroism throughout the history of the Metropolitan Police Service than I could ever fully tell. Police officers are on the streets day and night, trying to make London a safer place – without knowing what situation they will be faced with next. Yet they still tell me that they do not want to see every police officer routinely armed – and I agree. To maintain this position it is absolutely essential that we have a robust armed response system that can react swiftly to incidents across London round the clock. It's an issue we can never afford to be complacent about and we keep the situation and threat level under constant review – you cannot do otherwise when the safety of police officers is paramount. As a service, we have not reached the point where there is a need to arm all our officers – and I personally hope we never will.'

Lifting the siege

The Met is the national police training body for hostage and kidnap incidents and the Hostage and Crisis Negotiations Unit today provides specially trained negotiators for hostage and kidnap crimes in progress and for suicide prevention.

The one-hundredth hostage training course at Hendon was held in February 2004, marking 28 years of hostage negotiation in the Service. This area of expertise is now recognised around the world and the Met responds to requests from the Foreign and Commonwealth Office for assistance in cases involving British subjects. The Service has an advisory role in such incidents – it does not get involved with the negotiations on the ground, although it has played a large part in helping to free hostages held by the Khmer Rouge in Cambodia and those taken by militant groups and militias in the Middle East and Africa.

At any one time the Met has around 60 trained negotiators. Twelve are co-ordinators who are on 24-hour call. The incidents they cover include protesters who put themselves in dangerous situations, such as the Fathers for Justice group who have climbed cranes to draw attention to the plight of separated or divorced men denied access to their children. Negotiators will also be called in to talk down people attempting to commit suicide and 'trapped' criminals in siege situations.

The origin of the Met's siege expertise was during the international outbreak of politically motivated hijackings and kidnappings in the early 1970s. The then Commissioner Sir Robert Mark ordered a team of officers to draw up a plan to tackle such an incident should it occur in London. This plan swung into action for the first time at the so-called Spaghetti House siege in 1975. On September 28, three armed men attempted to rob the managers of the Spaghetti House restaurant in Knightsbridge of the day's takings, which totalled £13,000. While the robbers were ushering the restaurant staff down to the basement at gunpoint, one managed to escape and raise the alarm.

The Met was now faced with the type of siege situation they had been preparing for with specialist training. That incident set the tone for what has become a classic police siege strategy, summed up in three words – isolate, contain and negotiate. This allows officers to buy time for the hostages and consider all the options. Attempts were made to conduct hi-tech surveillance without the gunmen's knowledge. The men had demanded safe release and an aircraft to fly them abroad, but radio reports set out to lower the morale of the gunmen with reports that their demands would never be met. The Met managed to suppress a newspaper story that an associate of Franklin Davies, the leader of gang, had been arrested by police. It also channelled a hoax message to Davies informing him that the associate had sold his information to the press, which further undermined the gunmen's morale. For six days Met officers patiently talked to the gunmen, eventually persuading them to surrender and release the hostages unharmed. Although Davies claimed the gang were members of the Black Liberation Front, the Spaghetti House siege was regarded as a simple robbery that had gone wrong.

There was an extensive debriefing after the

Spaghetti House operation and the lessons learned were used a few months later in another West London siege. This time, however, there was no doubt about the politically motivated violence of the hostage-takers.

Between October 1974 and December 1975 a four-man IRA active service unit wrought havoc on the streets of London. While operational they were responsible for 50 terrorist incidents, including bombings of popular restaurants, shootings of prominent public figures and kidnappings. Their crimes claimed 11 victims, including Roger Goad, a bomb disposal officer, TV personality Ross McWhirter and the cancer specialist Hamilton Fairley (see chapter five).

An intelligence-led operation was launched by the Met to calculate the time and location of future attacks. Scott's restaurant in Mayfair was correctly identified as a target so when the IRA team drove past the restaurant on December 6, 1975 the police were waiting for them. The terrorists were pursued to Balcombe Street where they ran into a flat and took a couple hostage. Electronic surveillance equipment was used to monitor the terrorists' movements inside the

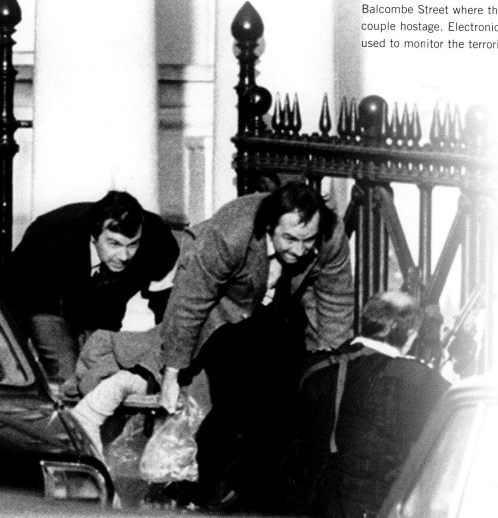

Left Plain clothes officers carry away the body of a hostage shot by terrorists during the 1980 Iranian Embassy siege. The threat of more killings triggered the storming of the Embassy by the SAS.

flat while Peter Imbert (later to become a Met Commissioner) negotiated with the terrorists. A consultant psychiatrist was also deployed to assess the mental state of those inside the flat.

In view of the string of violent attacks committed by the terrorists, the SAS were placed on standby and the site was screened from television and news cameras so that an element of surprise could be sustained. After six days, the IRA men surrendered.

The Iranian and Libyan Embassy sieges

One of the few occasions the Met has failed to bring a peaceful end to a hostage negotiation was during the Iranian Embassy siege in 1980, when the SAS were called in after the six gunmen who had stormed the embassy killed one of the hostages.

PC Trevor Lock, a Diplomatic Protection Group officer who was trapped in the embassy by the terrorists, received the George Medal for his bravery during the siege. Despite being searched by the gunmen, he had managed to conceal his handgun under his uniform and acted as a constant point of reassurance for the hostages and the gunmen. At one point he told the terrorists, 'The police will not attack you as long as you do not hurt or kill any hostages. They will wait 10 years if they have to, if it would mean a peaceful end to the siege with no bloodshed.'

His tireless patience, though, was not rewarded by everyone coming out of the Embassy alive. Despite the Met's dogged determination to end it peacefully, public memories of the siege will always be dominated by the ruthless efficiency of the SAS's storming operation. They killed five of the terrorists and successfully freed all of the hostages.

Four years later, London was once again the focus of terrorist violence at an international mission, but the incident that sparked the 10-day siege of the Libyan embassy in St James's Square is etched on the

Above WPC Yvonne Fletcher was shot dead in April 1984 as she helped police a demonstration outside the Libyan People's Bureau.

collective memory of the Metropolitan Police. WPC Yvonne Fletcher, 25, was, at just over five feet (1.5 m) in height, said to be the smallest police officer in Britain when she was shot dead outside the Libyan People's Bureau on April 17, 1984. She had been sent with other officers to St James's Square to police a demonstration by Libyan dissidents protesting against Colonel Gadaffi's regime.

As WPC Fletcher policed the demonstration she was shot in the back and mortally wounded by one of a series of bullets fired from the Libyan People's Bureau. The jury at the inquest ruled that she was 'unlawfully killed' by a bullet fired from a first-floor window, which may have been intended for one of the demonstrators. WPC Fletcher's murder led to a 10-day siege of the Embassy. Following intense diplomatic discussions the siege was brought to an end when it was agreed that all of the occupants of the Libyan People's Bureau, including those involved in the shooting, could leave the premises and be deported from the UK. While this action ensured the safe return of British citizens and diplomats from Libya, it prevented a thorough police investigation into the murder of WPC Fletcher as the suspects and any witnesses could not be interviewed.

The murder of a Met policewoman provoked widespread public anger, reflected in the editorial columns of one newspaper which suggested that the public good would have been better served by the sound of stun grenades and the sight of men in black balaclavas entering the building. WPC Fletcher's murder also led to the creation of the Police Memorial Trust, an organisation dedicated to placing public memorials at the locations of fallen officers.

In 1999 a diplomatic breakthrough was achieved when the Libyan government accepted 'general responsibility' for the events of 17 April, 1984. In 2004, ongoing diplomatic negotiations opened the way for an agreement that a joint investigation, under Libyan law, would be conducted into the death of WPC Fletcher, led by a Libyan examining magistrate and a detective chief superintendent from the Metropolitan Police Service.

The Hackney Siege

The longest-ever siege on mainland Britain took place on Boxing Day in Hackney in 2003 after a lone gunman, Eli Hall, 32, took a hostage and refused to surrender for 15 days. The siege was triggered when officers went to look at a suspect vehicle that had been identified in connection with an earlier shooting in Soho. When police tried to remove the vehicle, Hall leaned out of a window of a nearby flat and fired shots at them. Police believe Hall had at least two firearms in the building, some ammunition and a quantity of petrol. Officers at the scene also feared he had booby-trapped the building. During the course of the siege Hall opened fire at officers on six occasions.

The Hackney siege accounted for a significant level of Met resources and led to considerable disruption to the residents who lived in the area, which had to be

sealed off. The operation cost more than £700,000 and people were either asked to stay in their homes during the siege or were evacuated and alternative accommodation found for them in nearby hotels. As the siege wore on, the public started to ask why the police did not go into the building and bring the incident to a conclusion, but under Article 2 of the Human Rights Act the police have a statutory duty to preserve life, which meant that the Met sought a peaceful resolution to the siege and was not prepared to risk storming the building. During the siege, the Met used independent advisors at a tactical level. They also deployed a large number of intermediaries, including relatives and friends, to try and talk the gunman round.

Chair of the Independent Advisory Group, Claudine Duberry, said their independent role was very important in helping residents and shopkeepers to understand what the police were doing and why. Home beat officers worked 24 hours a day with Hackney Council's emergency planning team to keep people informed and reassure them. The Met also delivered medicines and food to residents trapped inside the cordon.

The hostage managed to break out of the building after 11 days but the Met was still playing a game of

Left CCTV footage showing a gang trying to smash its way through security glass in an attempt to steal the 203-carat Millennium Star, the world's largest diamond, in November 2000. The robbers used a JCB digger (far left) to crash through the outer wall of the Millennium Dome, but due to a carefully planned surveillance operation, police officers were waiting in ambush.

patience. After 15 days a fire was started in the building and officers were forced to enter the flat, where they found Hall's body. A formal public inquest into Hall's death is planned for January 2005.

After the siege ended, around 150 residents attended a public meeting at the council to air their views. Several had been restricted to their homes, others had not been able to return to theirs. Most people accepted that the Met had a duty of care to ensure the safety of those in the vicinity of the siege and also to end it peacefully. This view was summed up by Diane Abbott, MP for Hackney North and Stoke Newington. 'I support the way the police handled the situation,' she said. 'I do not think they had an alternative – the only other option would have been to burst in there and riddle him full of bullets.'

The Flying Squad

One of the best-known units in the Metropolitan Police, the Flying Squad was the first cross-border mobile police response in this country. In 1919 its use of vehicles and fast communications (Morse code) were cutting edge, and while the equipment and vehicles have been updated, the aims and remit of the modern-

day Flying Squad remain much the same.

Throughout its history the Squad has cemented its reputation by dealing extremely effectively with armed robbers and using informants to undermine gangs' activities. Squad officers have also identified and then acted against a succession of attempts by criminals to affect the outcomes of trials by intimidating or offering bribes to juries. It cleared up the £26 million Brinks Mat gold-bullion robbery and ended the reign of the most powerful London gang since the Krays and Richardsons, the south London Arifs.

During the 1970s and 1980s armed robberies involving banks and cash-in-transit vehicles had become a major problem in London. The gangs were gaining the upper hand and a tougher police response was required. Through the use of informants, Squad officers were able to mount a number of operations where they caught robbery gangs in the act, using firearms officers from the SO19 branch as armed back-up.

Flying Squad officers have dealt with London's most ruthless villains, and one Squad officer was the victim of the first machine-gun attack on a police officer in Britain. In 1993, Flying Squad Detective Sergeant

Michael Stubbs was in the back seat of a police car chasing armed robbers Steven Farrer and Anthony Pendrigh when one of 20 rounds fired from a Czech C25 submachine-gun came through the windscreen and grazed his head. Farrer and Pendrigh pleaded guilty to armed robbery, firearms charges and having a machine-gun with intent to resist arrest. They were each sentenced to 18 years by an Old Bailey judge.

The emergence of the National Crime Squad to tackle serious organised crime has raised questions about the role of the Flying Squad. During the early 1990s there were suggestions in the media that the Met was considering disbanding the Squad altogether. Flying Squad officers are, however, highly skilled detectives, trained in surveillance, the use of firearms and equipped with excellent vehicles.

Three 'levels' of crime are recognised by the police:
- level one – street level, within one borough (or police border);
- level two – cross-borough/borders (e.g. London-wide);
- level three – with national or international implications/relevance.

'The Flying Squad are there to pick up level 2 and level 3 criminals, as well as armed robbers,' says Deputy Assistant Commissioner Griffiths. 'The Squad is much more flexible now and fits in with the requirements of the National Intelligence Model' (the principles around which serious crime is investigated).

The National Intelligence Model provides a uniform standard for the way intelligence is collected by all police services in the UK so that they can develop an accurate picture of crime and target resources in the right way. This is more commonly known as intelligence-led policing. The model also allows police to track crime across different geographical areas and criminal justice agencies. It recognises that modern criminals do not restrict their activities to one particular type of crime or jurisdiction. So, for example, while the Flying Squad has been highly successful at tackling armed robbery, some of its traditional target criminals have moved into other areas such as drug trafficking, which can be more lucrative. But it would be a mistake to think that the problem of armed robbery has simply disappeared.

The Millennium Dome robbery

The Flying Squad remains a 'headline grabber' and continues to pull off some of the most spectacular operations in the Met's history. The attempted Millennium Dome Robbery on November 7, 2000 was a classic Met ambush of armed criminals. The target for the armed gang was £200 million in De Beers diamonds in an exhibition vault on display at the Millennium Dome. The jewels included the 203-carat Millennium Star – the word's biggest diamond. But when the robbers stormed into the Dome – crashing through the wall with a JCB digger – more than a hundred officers were waiting in ambush. The robbers, who were armed with sledgehammers, a nail gun, ammonia and smoke grenades, were stopped inches from the vault.

Had the raid succeeded, it would have been the biggest robbery in UK history, but a months-long surveillance operation mounted by Flying Squad officers had tracked the gang's every move. As a precautionary measure, the police substituted the most valuable gems – including the Millennium Star – with fakes.

Even seasoned detectives were shocked by the scale and ambition of the attempted robbery, which was committed in broad daylight at a public venue and involved the use of speedboats parked on the Thames as get-away vehicles. Commissioner Sir John Stevens said, 'Their efforts to pull off this robbery not just in broad daylight but in such a public place were utterly audacious – like something from a James Bond film.'

Above The Diplomatic Protection Group provides armed uniformed protection at London's embassies, high commissions and consulates.

Fifteen police officers and civilian staff who took part in the operation were later given commendations for bravery by the Commissioner. Later, Anthony Oppenheimer, President of De Beers Diamond Trading Company at the time of the attempted robbery, presented a replica Millennium Star to New Scotland Yard as a token of the company's appreciation. It now has a permanent home in the Met's Crime Museum. De Beers also made donations to Victim Support and the Met Voluntary Fund.

VIP protection and security

There are now three separate departments that perform protection duties – SO14, responsible for royalty protection, SO16, responsible for diplomatic protection, and SO17, which looks after the Houses of Parliament.

SO14, the Royalty Protection Operational Command Unit, has responsibility for the protection of the Monarch and other members of the Royal family. This is provided by personal protection officers and close protection officers. The unit also provides static protection at Royal residences and includes the Special Escort Group – highly trained motorcyclists who provide convoy protection for VIP vehicles and for high-speed transported loads such as bullion. They clear a path

through traffic for the vehicles under their protection and are also expert at defensive techniques to protect vehicles if they come under attack.

Under the Vienna Convention 1961, the Metropolitan Police has responsibility for the protection of London's sizeable diplomatic community. The SO16 Diplomatic Protection Group provides armed uniformed protection at London's embassies, high commissions and consulates. It also guards 10 Downing Street and the Palace of Westminster, as well as being on duty at ceremonial occasions such as the State Opening of Parliament. The static protection officers are backed up by mobile units that patrol central London's embassy areas and are able to provide an armed response if necessary.

Protection officers do joint training based around a national protection officer training course. Officers are also taught anti-hijacking techniques – a situation that actually occurred when gunmen attempted to kidnap Princess Anne in the Mall in 1974. All personal protection officers are also highly trained in first aid and can therefore take immediate action should the VIP they are protecting get injured. A major part of the training also involves negotiating and planning protection for VIPs in advance of state visits and other events, as one of the most important aspects of the job is risk assessment to ensure the safety of their charges.

SO17 is responsible for the security of the Palace of Westminster. Their role is to ensure a safe and secure environment on the Parliamentary Estate for MPs, peers, employees and the public.

As well as the other protection and security units, Special Branch has a role in the protection of high-profile individuals. Their highly trained 'A Squad' officers provide personal protection for prominent individuals who may be at risk from terrorist or other type of attack. These include UK nationals such as the Prime Minister and those at a similar level of risk who are visiting the UK from abroad.

5 Terrorism

London's police service, like its population, has a unique experience of living with the threat of terrorism. In this respect, the capital city and its everyday services have developed a resilience and expertise that are probably unrivalled in the Western world. London has been the target of international terrorism since 1969, while attacks by Irish extremists date back even further to the 1880s. Because of this the Metropolitan Police has developed specialist capabilities – principally housed within Special Branch, the Anti-Terrorist Branch and other units – that take a national and international lead in the fight against terrorism.

Specialist units play a vital role but undoubtedly the whole of the Met provides a response to terrorism, and every officer and member of police staff carries that responsibility. In the recent past, for example, uniformed officers on routine patrol have intercepted lorry bombs and cars containing terrorists armed with AK47 machine-guns before they reached their targets. The threat from Al-Qaeda and its associated groups has widened that responsibility to every conceivable agency, in both the public and private sectors, that makes a contribution towards London's security. Today the Met's response to terrorism is part of a highly sophisticated multi-agency approach to a global threat.

Left The devastation caused by a Provisional IRA car bomb left outside an army building in Whitehall in 1973.

The Angry Brigade and the 'Bomb Squad'

Thirty years ago the threat may have been more definable but attacks in London were frequent and deadly. The threat posed by the IRA and its successor, the Provisional IRA (PIRA), was met with a co-ordinated police response.

Although the IRA's origins date back to the early part of the 20th century, PIRA did not emerge as a potent force on the British mainland until 1973. Yet the trigger for a specialised anti-terrorist unit did not come from Irish Republican extremism but from international anarchists. In the late 1960s, James Christie, a self-confessed anarchist imbued with an anti-Franco fixation, joined a group of Spanish émigrés calling themselves the First of May Group. Between March 1968 and October 1970, 22 bomb attacks attributed to the group occurred in Europe. Twelve of these attacks were targeted on London and other parts of the UK. In 1970 Christie formed an alliance with a group of extreme left-wing students and they re-emerged as the Angry Brigade. The new group shifted its targets from supporters of General Franco to more conventional establishment figures in the UK. Bomb attacks against the Metropolitan Police Commissioner, the Attorney General, the Miss World contest and the Ministry of Employment culminated on January 12, 1971 when two sizable acid-delayed time bombs were planted against the home of Cabinet Minister, Robert Carr.

In December 1970, a small unit of Special Branch was ordered to look at all incidents of politically motivated crime. Shortly after the bombing of Robert Carr, 10 CID detectives and Special Branch officers formed an investigating team which became the first 'Bomb Squad'.The impact of the bombing on the Minister's home was enormous and a major inquiry was launched. A month later a breakthrough was achieved and two of the Angry Brigade activists were arrested.

The group responded by stepping up their bombing campaign and new clockwork time bombs were planted at yet more targets, including the Ford Motor Company, and a Territorial Army recruiting centre.

The Angry Brigade's campaign was brought to an end in August 1971 by the capture by the Bomb Squad of the leading members and their arsenal in a north London house. They were found in possession of explosives, detonators, machine-guns, ammunition and a mountain of documentary evidence on their past and future activities. Five defendants out of 12 were convicted at the Central Criminal Court in December 1972 in the largest criminal trial ever held in Britain, and were sentenced to 10 years' imprisonment. The judge praised the Bomb Squad officers for 'exorcising the evil from within our midst'. From that point the Bomb Squad – and subsequently the Anti-Terrorist Branch – based its badge and emblem on a medieval ex-communication ceremony involving a bell, a book and a candle. Its motto also became 'Short on sleep, long on memory.' Subsequently, 14 members of the Angry Brigade, including four of the five already convicted, pleaded guilty to a gigantic fraud, which had subsidised their terrorist activities.

It was not until March 1, 1976 that the Bomb Squad officially became the Anti-Terrorist Branch (SO13). By that time the threat of Irish Republican terrorism on the British mainland had become a full-blown menace.

The fight against PIRA

Between October 1974 and December 1975 a four-man PIRA active service unit mounted a series of attacks in London before being cornered and captured at the Balcombe Street siege (see chapter four). While operational they were responsible for 50 terrorist incidents, encompassing bombings, shootings and kidnapping. Their crimes claimed 11 victims, including

Above Angry Brigade marchers in Shepherds Bush in 1972. The Angry Brigade, a group of extreme left-wing students, targeted establishment figures such as the Attorney General and the Metropolitan Police Commissioner.

TV personality Ross McWhirter, the cancer specialist Hamilton Fairley and Captain Roger Goad, an explosives officer. It was as a direct result of this period of PIRA activity that in 1974 the Met set up its Bomb Data Centre, one of the first of its kind in the world. The BDC – which has become a world leader – collates and analyses information about global terrorist attacks. In turn it co-ordinates the dissemination of this vital information to forces across the UK.

The second part of the PIRA active service unit's campaign in 1975 was astonishing for the speed and frequency with which they selected their targets and mounted their attacks. Their targets included high-class restaurants, bombs were left in garrison towns such as Caterham, Surrey and Aldershot, Hampshire, and politicians were singled out for assassination. Former Prime Minister Edward Heath was targeted twice.

On August 29 a booby-trap device was left in a shop at Kensington Church Street, west London. Explosives officer Captain Roger Goad attempted to defuse it, but it exploded, killing him instantly. The next day a bomb exploded in Holborn, and on the day of Captain Goad's funeral a bomb was placed under a table at the Hilton Hotel. It was positioned so that when the warning was phoned through, the bomb would explode, catching the occupants evacuating the building. Two guests were killed and 63 others injured.

On October 9 a bomb exploded at a bus stop at Green Park close to the Ritz Hotel, killing a young man waiting for a bus. On October 13 a bomb was defused at Locketts restaurant. This device was packed with 30 lb (13.6 kg) of nuts and bolts added as shrapnel. On the morning of October 23, in Campden Hill Square, Holland Park, Professor Hamilton Fairley noticed an object under the car of the MP Gordon Fraser. As Professor Fairley approached the vehicle with his dog, it exploded, killing him.

On October 29 a bomb exploded at an Italian restaurant in South Audley Street. On November 3 a booby-trapped device on a car exploded at Connaught Square and a bomb was defused under Edward Heath's car in Wilton Street six days later. On November 12 a 'throw bomb' was put into Scotts restaurant, Mayfair, killing one occupant and injuring 15 others. Six days later there was a similar attack on Waltons restaurant in which two people were killed and 19 injured. This attack was within 24 hours of the discovery of explosives at Albion Towers in Southampton.

On November 27 Mrs Rosemary McWhirter, the wife of the TV personality Ross McWhirter, who had just offered a reward for information leading to the arrest of the bomber, returned home in her car and was confronted by two gunmen. They made her hand over the keys of the car and ring the doorbell. The door was opened by her husband, who was promptly shot dead as his terrified wife rushed past him into the house.

On December 6 at around 10 p.m. the four-man team, using a stolen car, drove past Scotts restaurant, a target they had attacked once before, and fired a burst from an Armalite combat rifle at the windows. Armed Met officers pursued the terrorists by car to Balcombe Street in Marylebone where the terrorists entered the flat of a middle-aged couple and took them hostage. The ensuing siege lasted five days and 19 hours and

Below Norris McWhirter, the twin brother of the TV personality Ross McWhirter who was shot dead by PIRA gunmen in 1975, leaving St Paul's Cathedral after attending a memorial service for his brother.

police were able to put into effect the contingency plans developed during the Spaghetti House Siege (see chapter four) which brought to the fore the Met's negotiating expertise. The terrorists realised that a position of stalemate had been reached and there was no advantage to them in holding two elderly people, or harming them – so, having released their captives, they surrendered.

The four prisoners were identified as Harry Duggan, Edward Butler, Joseph O'Connell and Hugh Doherty.

The gun used in the McWhirter killing and the Armalite used to shoot up Scotts restaurant were recovered from the flat. Two safe houses containing weapons and explosive materials were later found at Crouch Hill and Milton Grove. There was also enough forensic evidence to link the suspects to a number of terrorist incidents, including a bombing in Aldershot, Hamsphire in December 1974 in which five people were killed. It was at these two houses that the team made up their bombs and where their seemingly normal everyday life did not make them stand out among the large number of bedsit tenants who lived in the area. They left their houses every day as if to go to work, were neat and tidy in appearance and moderate in their drinking habits. They also paid the rent regularly. The gang brought the explosives and weapons used in the attacks over from Ireland. To travel to and from their targets they used the Underground and stolen Ford cars.

In the two-year period during which this prolific active service unit was at large, the Provisional IRA also murdered a Met police officer, but it would be 13 years before the killer was brought to justice. At the time he was killed, PC Stephen Tibble was 21, with a 19-year-old wife, and had spent only six months in the police service. On February 26, 1975, he was dressed in jeans and an anorak and riding his 175 cc Honda motorcycle when he witnessed an incident in Hammersmith, just a minute after leaving home. A man being questioned by three plain clothes officers broke away and ran. As a chase began, PC Tibble revved up his motorbike, caught up with the suspect and jumped off to tackle him. In the struggle that followed, three shots were fired, two hitting PC Tibble in the chest. Leaving the officer dying on the ground, the gunman fled towards Barons Court underground station.

A large-scale manhunt ensued but the killer escaped arrest. The Met later discovered the identity of the man – William Joseph Quinn, a senior PIRA operative who was running a bomb factory only 300 yards (275 metres) from where PC Tibble had been shot dead. Quinn had made the bombs in the basement of No. 39 Fairholme Road, West Kensington, and it was thought that he was on his way back to the house when he was surprised by Met detectives who wanted to question him as part of a routine inquiry into a series of local burglaries.

Quinn was arrested in Dublin in April 1975 and convicted of being an IRA member. The Met had already pinpointed him as the young officer's killer, but an extradition dispute between Ireland and Britain allowed Quinn to go free in 1976. Having been born in the USA, Quinn returned there in 1979 and worked as a clerk in a relative's stationery supply firm in Dale City.

Quinn was finally arrested in San Francisco in October 1981 by the FBI. The Met had to settle for charging Quinn with PC Tibble's murder but dropping the terror charges because defence lawyers successfully exploited a legal loophole, arguing in the US courts that he had been charged too long after the offences had been committed. After a unique five-year extradition struggle with the United States, Quinn stood trial at the Old Bailey. The presiding judge, Mr Justice Rose, told him, 'You shot repeatedly and at point-blank range a man who was in fact a police officer, though you could not have known he was other than an ordinary member of the public. It was an appalling cold-blooded killing, untinged by any remorse on your part, and motivated no doubt by the terrorist activities on which at that time you were engaged.' Quinn, 40, was sentenced to life imprisonment on February 16, 1988.

PC Tibble was the first police victim of PIRA's mainland terrorism campaign. Two explosives officers also lost their lives, both to 5 lb (2.5 kg) PIRA bombs: Captain Roger Goad in 1975 and Ken Howarth in

October 1981, who was killed by an explosion while attempting to defuse a bomb that had been left at a Wimpy Bar in Oxford Street. The Met lost three other officers to a PIRA bomb explosion outside Harrods in December 1983. Inspector Stephen Dodd, Sergeant Noel Lane and WPC Jane Arbuthnot were killed as they approached a car packed with explosives. A police dog handler, PC John Gordon, lost both his legs in the explosion, and three members of the public were killed while 90 other people were injured.

Political assassinations

Over the three decades that Irish Republican extremists have committed acts of violence on the British mainland, their range of targets has varied considerably. Significant economic locations, such as the Square Mile and the Docklands development (see below), have featured high on the terrorists' hit list, but prominent political and public figures have also been the focus of assassination attempts.

Margaret Thatcher's Conservative government, which came to power in 1979 and adopted a hard line against Irish Republican extremism, was subject to a series of major attacks. In March 1979, on the eve of the general election that brought Mrs Thatcher into office, a parallel Republican group, the Irish National Liberation Army (INLA), planted a bomb under the car of shadow Northern Ireland Secretary Airey Neave. The bomb exploded as the MP was driving out of the House of Commons, killing him instantly. In 1984, the Anti-Terrorist Branch was involved in an investigation of an PIRA attack that came close to assassinating the British Prime Minister and most of her Cabinet. After the attack PIRA warned, 'We've only got to be lucky once, you have got to be lucky all the time.'

The explosion at the Grand Hotel in Brighton on October 12 at 2.42 a.m. killed five people and injured 31 others. At the time of the attack the hotel was

Above A receipt signed by the man suspected of planting the timed device in the Brighton hotel which almost resulted in the assassination of Margaret Thatcher and many of her Cabinet in 1984.

Right The aftermath of the Bishopsgate bomb in the City of London in 1993. A number of international banks considered moving to other European cities due to the PIRA threat in London.

being used by Prime Minister Margaret Thatcher and several members of her Cabinet, attending the Conservative Party Conference. The bomb detonated in the bathroom of room 629, and resulted in severe structural damage – including the demolition of all seven floors directly above the main entrance. One thousand tons of debris was removed from the scene for forensic examination. A mysterious 'Mr Walsh' had been the occupant of room 629 for four days in the middle of September 1984 and could well have planted an electronic timed device with a delay of several weeks. However, no evidence of the circuitry has been recovered to this day. The Provisional IRA claimed responsibility for the incident.

The terrorist attack in Brighton led directly to the formation of the Police National Search Centre in Kent and the creation of POLSAs – Police Search Advisors. POLSAs have become an integral part in the fight against terrorism and play a major role in crime reduction.

Bishopsgate and the 'ring of steel'

In the early 1990s PIRA stepped up its mainland campaign with a series of devastating attacks on London. On April 24, 1993 a telephoned bomb warning was received at Sky Television. The caller stated that a massive bomb had been planted in

Bishopsgate between Leadenhall Street and Hounsditch Road, and that it would go off in 40 minutes. Following this initial call a further 12 calls were received by a variety of agencies. An immediate search of the area revealed a blue tipper truck which was parked, unattended, facing south with its hazard warning lights operating. The area was evacuated, but a freelance photographer eluded the cordons and was close to the vehicle when the device exploded. He was killed and 34 other people were injured.

This had been a massive attack. The crater left by the explosion was 36 feet (11 metres) in diameter and 15 feet (4.6 metres) deep. Window damage extended over half a mile from the site of the explosion. Police at the scene recovered fragments of a battery holder, batteries and a snap connector. This suggested that there were possibly two timer and power units involved. The device contained inside the truck incorporated a very large charge of improvised explosive mixture with a mass of up to 6,500 lb (3,000 kg).

As a result of the Bishopsgate bomb and a later explosion at the Baltic Exchange, extensive security measures were put in place to protect the City of London's Square Mile, the site of London's financial institutions as well as international banking. The so-called 'ring of steel' severely restricted vehicle access to the Square Mile area. Armed police checkpoints on the edge of the barrier stopped vehicles as they entered and many were searched. These bombs were significant because a number of banks with offices in the area considered moving to other European cities. This would have been a blow not just for the job market in the UK but for the City's reputation as a financial centre of world renown. As economic targets go, the attacks could not have been more damaging.

Operation Excel

PIRA kept up the pressure and turned its attention to

another significant target. In March 1994, it launched three separate mortar attacks on Heathrow Airport, which caused great disruption to the public, considerable financial loss to the airport authority and attracted global media interest. The scenes of the three attacks were subject to full forensic recovery by the Anti-Terrorist Branch but no clues or intelligence as to the identity of the bombers were available.

However, a public appeal for information resulted in a significant call to the confidential Anti-Terrorist Hotline. The caller described suspicious activity in and around a garage in West Hampstead just prior to the bombings. Specifically he described a red Ford Sierra delivering large packages, work in the garage late at night and the laying of heavy plastic sheeting on the floor of the garage. The garage floor was swabbed for explosive traces and produced a positive result. Sweepings were then taken and full forensic examination conducted.

The Sierra had been purchased 19 days before the bombings and sold 25 days later, having been valeted, at a loss of £800. The car and its registration documents were recovered and forensically examined,

Left and above A major intelligence operation codenamed 'Airlines' led Anti-Terrorist officers to the basement of a house in south London in July 1996, where they discovered 37 bomb detonators fully charged and ready for use. These devices were intended for use against London's key power stations; had the attack been carried out, the capital city could have been left without electricity for months.

but the fingerprints found did not match any on the Anti-Terrorist Branch's database. The person who had rented the garage from the owner had given false details. But he was due to receive a £50 deposit refund from the owner and a full surveillance operation was launched on the garage should he return for the money. An individual named Michael Gallagher, posing as a Mr Fraser, eventually telephoned the owner and made arrangements with him to collect the down payment. Gallagher was covertly photographed, samples of his handwriting were obtained and he was then followed to his home address.

Michael Gallagher was subject to intensive surveillance for more than two years, in the hope of identifying other members of the PIRA active service unit. By that time PIRA had declared a ceasefire on its mainland bombing campaign and the Anti-Terrorist Branch, Special Branch and the intelligence services used the surveillance operation both to gather evidence against Gallagher and use him as a barometer for terrorist activity.

The ceasefire ended with the Docklands bombing in February 1996, and Gallagher was arrested in October

of that year. He was now forensically linked to the Sierra as his prints matched a palm print on the registration document. Fibres from the car, from the floor sweepings of the garage and of the two land-based mortar sites were compared and provided incontrovertible evidence linking all four sites. The eavesdropping tapes were converted into evidence, and voice analysis and handwriting analysis were also undertaken by experts, resulting in a formidable quantity of prosecution evidence.

Gallagher was the quartermaster for an active service unit and was essential to PIRA's campaign on the mainland. He told Anti-Terrorist Branch officers when they arrested him that 'there's not many people like me'. He was found guilty of conspiracy to cause explosions and sentenced to 20 years in February 1998.

Operation Excel underlined the vital role of public vigilance in the Met's efforts to defeat terrorism and showed the value of the confidential Anti-Terrorist hotline, which was launched in 1991. Information and intelligence given to the hotline has resulted in the arrest and conviction of a number of terrorists. Today, the Anti-Terrorist Hotline receives on average over 650 calls a month. John Grieve, head of the Anti-Terrorist Branch at the time of Operation Excel, coined the phrase, 'Communities defeat terrorism.'

Operation Airlines

Two of the most outstanding police successes against PIRA were Operations Airlines and Tinnitus. What marked out these two cases was that the Met was able to arrest and convict the terrorists before they carried out their attacks. Proactive work by Met officers, the RUC in Northern Ireland, the An Garda Síochána in the Irish Republic and British intelligence services meant that the police were one step ahead of the terrorists at every stage.

The head of the Anti-Terrorist Branch would later describe the attack halted by Operation Airlines as potentially the most significant terrorist incident in the UK since the Gunpowder Plot. PIRA's plan was to seriously disrupt the electricity supply of London. Had they achieved their aim, many parts of the capital would have been without electricity for up to several months. The terrorists had identified key power stations, had expert help and knew exactly where to plant the devices.

On July 15, 1996 eight men including Patrick Martin, Gerard Hanratty, Francis Rafferty, Robert Morrow, Donal Gannon and John Crawley were arrested at two south London addresses. The arrests were the culmination of an extensive, and well co-ordinated surveillance operation lasting eight days and involving around 300 officers from Special Branch, the Anti-Terrorist Branch and the Security Service. More than 25,000 hours of surveillance evidence was collected.

The PIRA active service unit was considered to be one of the most specialised, experienced, resourceful and highly motivated ever to have operated on the British mainland. John Crawley, for example, was a

Above Explosives seized from a storage unit in Hornsey, north London during Operation Tinnitus. Tinnitus was an example of how joint working between the security services was turning the tables on PIRA.

former US Marine and had served with Special Forces. At his trial, the USA sent over witnesses to give evidence against him.

Each member of the terrorist team also had a particular skill to offer. These ranged from practical skills such as carpentry and welding to military training, including intelligence gathering and surveillance. The suspects were seen during the surveillance operation to conduct reconnaissance of electricity supply stations around the M25. These sub-stations supplied all London's electricity needs. The suspects were also seen to make various purchases, which later transpired to be the components and equipment used to manufacture a type of time and power unit (TPU) or detonators not previously seen on the UK mainland.

When the houses, garage and vehicles used by the active service unit were searched by the Met, a vast amount of terrorist paraphernalia was found. The most significant find was in the basement of a house in Lugard Road, SE15, where 37 fully functional detonators were on charge, and available for deployment. The subsequent investigation established that the timers in the TPUs were set to activate during the early hours of a Monday morning.

Also found was detailed information about electrical sub-stations, a large collection of forged documents and other equipment, including maps, plans, sketches, cut-down ladders and tools. The terrorists were well financed and had access to around £56,000. Each member of the unit had procured up to four false identities, made up of fraudulently obtained or stolen passports, driving licences and identity cards.

Unusually, two members of the active service unit gave evidence at their trial at the Central Criminal Court. They both stated that they were members of PIRA and that they had been on a mission to plant hoax devices at the electrical sub-stations in what Hanratty described as the IRA's 'coup of the century'. The reality was more chilling. The jury was told that the active service unit's actual intention was to damage the transformers at the electrical sub-stations, leaving London without any electricity for months. The capital would have effectively ground to a halt. On July 2, 1997, Hanratty, Crawley, Morrow, Rafferty, Martin and Gannon were found guilty of conspiracy to cause explosions and each was sentenced to 35 years' imprisonment. The judge, Mr Justice Scott-Baker, in praising the operation, said the security forces were 'one jump ahead' of the terrorists.

Operation Tinnitus

In August 1996 the Metropolitan Police and Security Service jointly instigated a surveillance operation against five men believed to be members of a PIRA active service unit based in the Hammersmith area of West London. Codenamed Tinnitus, the operation was to become the largest and longest counter-terrorist surveillance operation conducted in England.

The suspects were observed for six weeks, during which time it was discovered that they were operating an elaborate means of communication with each other using pseudonyms and coded messages within a pager network. Two of the suspects, Kelly and McHugh, had taken up residence in a West London Hotel, having checked in under false names. The other members of the gang were London-based. Their activities included the collection of a lorry from Beighton near Sheffield.

This lorry was brought to London for the purpose of converting it to a vehicle-borne bomb to be placed and detonated against an unknown target. In addition the suspects were seen visiting the premises of a self-storage company in Hornsey, north London. At the storage warehouse, anti-terrorist officers discovered a unit being used by the suspects as an arsenal to store more than six tons of home-made explosives. A lot of this material was packed into large wooden crates, each with booster tubes and detonating cord, a quantity of Semtex, 25 time and power units, two under-car booby traps, 17 electric detonators and a large range of firearms, together with ammunition. Later in the inquiry a storage unit believed to be used by one of the suspects was found in which there was a holdall containing further amounts of Semtex and bomb-making equipment. The Semtex found at the two venues totalled 10 kg (22 lb). The quantity of explosives seized by police was sufficient to make three large vehicle bombs, each comparable to the size of those detonated at South Quay in London's Docklands and Manchester city centre in 1996.

On September 23 1996, Anti-Terrorist Branch officers, assisted by armed units from the Met and the City of London and Sussex Police Tactical Firearms teams, arrested Brian McHugh, Patrick Kelly, James Murphy and Michael Phillips. The fifth suspect, Diarmuid O'Neill, was shot by armed police during the course of arrest and subsequently died. The investigation had amassed 50,000 hours of surveillance evidence. Some 10,000 pages of

documents were served on the defence in addition to 7,000 pages of witness statements. Three of the four defendants, McHugh, Kelly and Murphy, were subsequently convicted at the Central Criminal Court of offences of possession of explosives and conspiracy to cause explosions. On December 16, 1997 they were sentenced to 25, 20 and 17 years' imprisonment respectively. The fourth defendant, Phillips, was acquitted.

The shattered peace

In the mid-1990s there was a brief lull in PIRA's mainland bombing campaign in the shape of an 18-month ceasefire. During this period Anti-Terrorist and Special Branch officers continued to gather intelligence on PIRA activity (see Operation Excel above) and it was clear that the terrorists had the men and the equipment in place to restart attacks as soon as they decided the ceasefire was no longer a tactic they wanted to pursue.

When the end to the ceasefire came on February 9, 1996, it was a massive statement of intent by PIRA. Just after 7 p.m. a huge explosion ripped through the heart of Docklands on the Isle of Dogs. The lorry bomb at South Quay killed two newsagents as they cashed up in their shop on Friday night while hundreds of office workers were injured by flying glass. The estimated cost of the damage was £150 million.

From this devastation the Anti-Terrorist Branch began the complex and meticulous Operation Heron, which involved working closely with the RUC and An Garda Síochána. It highlighted remarkable forensic skills and showed the importance of CCTV as an investigative tool. Through a painstaking gathering of

Left The destruction of South Quay, in London's Docklands. The attack in February 1996 marked the end of an 18-month ceasefire in PIRA's mainland bombing campaign, killing two.

evidence – including a massive fingertip search of the surrounding area – officers began to link the pieces together. An appeal to the public to come forward with information about the lorry bomb led to a vital call being made to the Met's Anti-Terrorist hotline. As a result police went to River Road in Barking and uncovered crucial evidence – again demonstrating how the police and public can work together to bring terrorists to justice.

At River Road police found a vehicle trailer, Irish number plates and a tyre, inside which was found tachographs, a trucking magazine, newspapers and other items. Extensive enquiries revealed that the vehicle had made two journeys to the mainland. The first, in January, had been a dummy run. The second journey was made on February 7, two days before the bombing. The investigation revealed that the driver had made overnight stops at a particular truck stop in Carlisle on both occasions. On the second trip that the vehicle was driven south, the journey was recorded on motorway surveillance cameras. A further stop was made at South Mimms and from there the vehicle went to River Road. It was here that two men were seen with the vehicle and using a nearby café. From River Road the lorry was driven to South Quay where security cameras appear to show two men leaving the vehicle prior to the explosion.

Met fingerprint experts examined four rooms at the truck stop in Carlisle. Among exhibits taken for forensic testing was a glass ashtray. The team also received a number of exhibits, including a trucking magazine and a number of ferry tickets for a return journey between Belfast and Stranraer. Among the latent 'marks' developed were three impressions of a right thumb. The significance of this tie-up showed that the same person had brought the vehicle over to the mainland on both occasions as the ferry ticket was dated January 16 and the room rented on February 8, 1996. The quality of

the mark developed on the ashtray was such that a search of the National Fingerprint Database could be undertaken. Over 350,000 responses were viewed on NAFIS (National Automated Fingerprint Identification System) with a negative result. The thumb print was also checked by the Scottish Criminal Records Office and the RUC's Fingerprint Bureau. As a result more than 180 suspects were put forward for comparison against 243 developed finger and palm marks.

The Anti-Terrorist Branch focused their attention on South Armagh where the vehicle had been converted into a lorry bomb and had begun its journey to the mainland. A number of people were arrested and brought over to London by Anti-Terrorist Branch officers, but none of those detained was the 'triple thumb print man'.

In April 1997 the RUC and units of the British Army arrested the members of a PIRA active service unit near Cullyhanna, South Armagh, in possession of a long-range sniper's rifle. Their fingerprints were taken and the RUC fingerprint bureau found a match between the latent thumb mark on the glass ashtray and the thumb print of James McArdle. Further comparison work revealed that a total of 14 marks from this operation were identical with McArdle's. These included marks on the ferry tickets, the truck stop registration form for the room where the glass ashtray had been found, the lorry park ticket and the trucking magazine, which had been bought in the Irish Republic.

At McArdle's first trial in February 1998 the jury was unable to return a verdict and a retrial was ordered. At the retrial, in June 1998, McArdle was found guilty for his part in the Docklands bombing but the jury was discharged from reaching a verdict on the charge of murder due to details published in a national newspaper the morning after the first verdict had been reached. Mr Justice Kay sentenced McArdle

to 25 years' imprisonment.

Nine days after the Docklands bombing, on February 18, 1996, an explosion destroyed a double-decker London Transport bus just after it had turned into the Aldwych. But this time it appeared that a PIRA attack had failed: the explosive device appeared to have gone off before it reached its intended target, taking the bomber's life. The dead man's injuries appeared consistent with him either carrying a device in a holdall or standing next to someone who was. A Walther P38 pistol was recovered lying a short distance from him on the road surface. A hole some 16 by 21 inches (40 by 53 cm) was found in the floor of the lower deck of the bus at a point just in front of the centre door in a place where a person getting off the bus would have stood. Twelve other people were injured in the explosion, some seriously, including the bus driver who was blown from his cab. The bus suffered severe damage, the roof having been almost ripped off and the upper deck blown apart. The extent of the wreckage would have

Above The wreckage of a double-decker bus in Aldwych caused by a bomb that seemingly detonated before it reached its intended target. The body of the probable bomber was thrown across the road, and 12 people were injured in the blast.

been consistent with a charge of high explosive equivalent to a 2.5 kg (5.5 lb) block of Semtex. The security services and police were never able to establish what the bomber's target was supposed to have been.

Successes in the fight against PIRA

In the space of four years the Met had scored major successes against PIRA, leading to the arrest and conviction of a number of its most experienced active service units. The police and Security Service had also managed to thwart several attacks, which, if they had gone ahead, would have caused considerable damage and disruption to London and loss of life.

Two key factors contributed to these successes.

Firstly, by the end of the 1980s it had become clear that there was a need for proper co-ordination of the UK policing effort, and that one police officer should be in overall command of UK terrorist investigations, with the authority to direct and co-ordinate all aspects of an investigation in all the police force areas affected. To meet this need, the Association of Chief Police Officers created a new role in 1990: National Co-ordinator for Terrorist Investigations. It was decided that this role should be fulfilled by the head of the Met's Anti-Terrorist Branch, which had the resources and expertise to take on such a responsibility. Secondly, active co-operation between the Met and other agencies had increased the range and scope of the investigations. The alliance between the Metropolitan Police, MI5, the RUC and the An Garda Síochána in the Republic of Ireland became known within security circles as a corporate brand – 'Counter-Terrorism PLC'.

In the past, rivalries between different agencies had prevented effective co-operation. Working relationships were now very good from top to bottom. For example, Met officers regularly made trips to Belfast and Dublin and stayed there for long periods, actively conducting investigations. This culminated in the Anti-Terrorist Branch conducting an operation in South Armagh for the first time in 25 years (see Operation Heron, page 107).

Operation Benedict was a classic example of effective co-operation between the Anti-Terrorist Branch, Security Service, the An Garda Síochána and the FBI. As a result of this operation three senior members of the Real IRA (the dissident Irish Republican group that committed the Omagh bomb outrage in August 1998 which killed 29 people) each received sentences of 30 years for conspiracy to cause explosions and other terrorism-related offences. During the course of this operation and subsequent trial, a number of landmark firsts were achieved, including:

- the first successful prosecution of Irish Republican terrorists under the Terrorism Act 2000;
- the first time Irish Republican terrorists had been prosecuted for an offence committed outside the UK;
- the first international 'sting' prosecution brought by the Anti-Terrorist Branch and the Security Service.

The operation began with information from an American agent who was jointly controlled by the Garda and the FBI, and latterly the Security Service. This agent had penetrated the heart of the Real IRA – a hard-line splinter group that had separated itself from PIRA after the Good Friday peace agreement in Northern Ireland. He provided information that the Real IRA was in need of funds and weaponry and the Anti-Terrorist Branch was introduced to exploit the evidential opportunities. As a result, Security Service agents purporting to be Iraqi agents lured the subjects to meetings in Eastern Europe with the promise of providing arms and funding. All meetings were recorded. It was after one such meeting, and with the full co-operation of the Slovakian authorities, that Slovakian police arrested the three on the authority of warrants issued in the UK to the Anti-Terrorist Branch. Extradition was granted and all three were brought back to the UK to stand trial. The outcome took three senior members of the Real IRA out of circulation and virtually paralysed the organisation at a time when it was planning to greatly extend its operations and capability.

The Anti-Terrorist Branch also developed systems for converting very complicated and sensitive intelligence into evidence that could be put before the courts. Scene examination and the use of intricate and painstaking searches, carried out by police POLSA teams, produced some startling results. For example, following the Docklands bomb in February 1996 detectives decided to close about three miles of road in east London, effectively shutting down the whole of the East End. They organised a fingertip search along this road, which led to the discovery of documents and fingerprints relating to the man responsible for the attack. This fingertip search was carried out by relay after relay of officers (literally hundreds were involved) and was similar to searching through a three-mile rubbish tip. Officers working on terrorism cases also became acutely aware of the dangers of contamination of evidence.

CCTV

The proliferation of CCTV in the UK has undoubtedly provided anti-terrorist officers with a vital new investigative tool.

Operation Studio is an example of a highly successful joint operation by the MPS Anti-Terrorist Branch, West Midlands and West Yorkshire Police and police services in northern and southern Ireland, in which evidence gathered from CCTV footage played a major role. James Patrick McCormack, John Hannan, Noel Maguire, Robert Hulme and Aiden Hulme were convicted in April 2003 for their role in two bomb attacks in London and one in Birmingham. All of the terrorists were given sentences ranging between 16 and 22 years.

The car bomb attacks took place outside the BBC Television Centre and at Ealing Broadway in London, and in Queensway, Birmingham in 2001. Miraculously, only a small number of people suffered minor injuries, despite the scant information given to police before the explosions. Authenticated coded telephone warnings for the bombs failed to give precise details about the types of vehicles involved, their location or time of detonation. In Birmingham

Above Extraordinary CCTV footage of a Real IRA bomb exploding in Ealing in August 2001. Evidence secured from surveillance cameras once again proved vital in the police investigation.

police were given only 30 minutes to respond.

DAC Peter Clarke, head of the MPS Anti-Terrorist Branch, said after the case, 'The bombs were put in busy areas where hundreds of people were either working or enjoying themselves on an evening out. It was nothing short of a miracle that we were not dealing with large numbers of dead and injured. The warnings given by the bombers were vague and misleading.'

CCTV was central to police enquiries, and helped detectives to plot the bombers' movements both prior to and in the aftermath of the attacks. Hundreds of hours of footage were retrieved and scanned by officers. As always, information from members of the public was also vital, and a media appeal for information gave police a significant breakthrough. In August 2001 police released an e-fit of the man who had bought the Ealing bomb car, along with CCTV footage of the driver. A 73-year-old housewife recognised one of the men and contacted police. She said that he looked like someone who had recently moved into a house in Cornwallis Avenue, Edmonton.

Enquiries revealed that Noel Maguire, a secondhand car dealer from Northern Ireland, had been renting the house since June 2001. On 15 November Anti-Terrorist Branch officers swooped on the address and arrested him. He was taken to Paddington Green Police Station, and made no comment throughout his interview.

Through their enquiries into Maguire's activities, the Met discovered that Maguire and the other defendants were involved in illegal 'diesel washing' to fund their terrorist activities. Diesel washing involves removing the red dye in agricultural diesel to turn it into the purer white diesel. With the red dye washed out using chemicals and filters, the white diesel can be sold at enormous profit. Maguire and his associates had been involved in diesel washing in Nottinghamshire and Humberside, before moving their operations to a barn at a farm in Yorkshire in May 2001. The gang then rented a house at another farm half a mile away.

The farm was raided by police on November 15, 2001. A Silver Vauxhall Cavalier was searched, and a holdall containing a Smith and Wesson revolver plus three rounds of ammunition seized from the boot. The holdall also revealed electric detonators, a hand grenade and an improvised timing device. The device was identical to the one used in the attack in Birmingham. A crucial find was also made within the

Above A court artist's sketch of Mardi Gra bomber Edgar Pearce and his brother Ronald. Edgar Pearce pleaded guilty to 20 counts of demanding money with menaces and other offences during a three-year terror campaign.

farmhouse. Police already knew that the coded telephone warning before the Birmingham bombing had been made from a mobile phone purchased in Waltham Cross in September 2001. The box for the phone was found inside the farmhouse, and the fingerprints of Robert Hulme, James McCormack and John Hannan were on it. The fingerprints of all five defendants were found at various points inside the farmhouse. Police also recovered a mobile phone belonging to Aiden Hulme. Examination of the SIM card revealed vital evidence that linked Aiden Hulme to the Ealing bomb. Just 12 hours after the blast Hulme's phone had received a text message depicting fizzling sticks of dynamite and the words 'Up the Provos'. Minutes later, a further message was sent which read, 'What were U at last night Hi Huh Hi Huh?' Whoever sent the messages believed Hulme had been involved in the bombing the night before. When Hulme was later arrested, the phone number he asked police to contact on his behalf was the same number as that used to send these text messages.

Police also uncovered mobile phone evidence linking Maguire to the BBC taxi bomb. Cell site enquiries showed that a particular mobile phone was being used along the route taken by the taxi on the evening of the blast. The phone was not used again until just after the explosion. The number of that mobile phone was later found in the possession of two associates of Noel Maguire, written or stored next to Maguire's nickname – B.D. Enquires also showed that on the night of the explosion the phone had been in regular contact with a mobile phone belonging to a man called John King, an alias regularly used by Aiden Hulme and the name he gave officers on arrest. The manufacturer's box for the phone used to make the coded warnings for the Birmingham car bomb was found at a farm in Yorkshire. It contained the fingerprints of Robert Hulme, James McCormack and John Hannan. The phone itself was never recovered.

At the scene of the Birmingham bomb, West Midlands police recovered fragments from a black fleece jacket. Forensic evidence showed that the jacket had been in the boot next to the bomb, and possibly even wrapped around it. Fibres from this fleece were later found by police during forensic searches of the farm in Yorkshire. They were also discovered in the Land Rover used by the suspects to travel to the UK the day before the Birmingham bomb, and in the Peugeot driven by John Hannan on the day of his arrest. A Land Rover parked at McCormack's home address was found to contain fibres identical to those found on the fleece at the scene of the Birmingham explosion. This fleece also revealed DNA belonging to James McCormack.

After the trial DAC Peter Clarke commented, 'This was a huge and meticulous investigation. Over 40,000 documents were put in evidence, and more than 8,000 CCTV tapes examined. It was like a giant jigsaw, but in the end produced a compelling picture of the terrorist plot.'

Non-political acts of terror

Occasionally the Metropolitan Police has been called on to investigate acts of terror that are carried out by no recognisable political group. In some ways, such cases are harder to investigate than conventional terrorist campaigns as police are often dealing with individuals who are either motivated by personal hatred or greed, have no known background and act in an unpredictable way. Two recent cases were the nail bomber David Copeland (see chapter four) and the Mardi Gra bomber.

Edgar Pearce, a former advertising agent, mounted a letter-bomb campaign over a three-year period between 1994 and 1997 aimed at extorting money from Barclays Bank and the Sainsbury's supermarket chain. Pearce adopted the pseudonym 'Mardi Gra' and used a threatening logo of four men wearing dark suits and sunglasses copied from the film *Reservoir Dogs*. He used it both to identify devices and ransom demands sent by him and to promote a sense of fear in the community.

Pearce's commercial terrorism campaign commenced on December 6, 1994, with the postal delivery of six improvised devices to six different branches of Barclays Bank. Pearce eventually planted or posted a total of 26 devices aimed at Barclays, followed by extortion demands between December 1994 and April 1996. His last 11 devices, from November 15, 1997, were all directed at Sainsbury's. In all, nine demands for money were intermixed with the letter and parcel bombs, but the eighth demand, in which Pearce dictated the method of pay-off, proved to be his downfall. At the request of the Mardi Gra Bomber, thousands of plastic cards bearing the Sainsbury's web address were circulated inside the April 23 edition of *Exchange & Mart* magazine. These cards were, in fact, capable of operating as cash cards at hundreds of ATM machines across the UK.

A combined operation involving the Anti-Terrorist Branch, the Organised Crime Group, other Met specialist departments and the National Crime Squad was launched to catch the bomber. A crucial part of the inquiry was a major surveillance operation at numerous cash-withdrawal machines situated at banks in and around London. On April 28, 1998 Pearce was arrested while attempting to obtain cash from an ATM in Whitton, West London. Also arrested was his elder brother Ronald, who later pleaded guilty at the Central Criminal Court of unlawfully possessing an electric stun gun and received a custodial sentence of 12 months.

Pearce admitted that he was the Mardi Gra Bomber and was jailed for 21 years. He pleaded guilty to 20 counts of demanding money with menaces, explosives offences and possession of firearms.

International terrorism

London is a major diplomatic centre and acts as a base for national, ethnic and cultural representative groups. Its long-standing tolerance of political protest and debate have also attracted unwelcome attention from those wishing to pursue their objectives through violent means. The Iranian and Libyan Embassy sieges in 1980 and 1984 respectively (see chapter four) demonstrated the potential of that threat and Middle-Eastern terrorism has re-emerged on London's streets in more recent times.

On July 26, 1994, the Washington Peace Declaration was signed by Prime Minister Rabin of Israel and King Hussein of Jordan, paving the way for peace between the two countries. But while the world was celebrating progress towards peace in the Middle East, extremists who were opposed to the agreement targeted Israeli and Jewish interests in London. Just after midday a bomb exploded in an Audi outside the Israeli Embassy in Kensington, causing substantial damage to the Embassy and other buildings. Astonishingly, no one was killed, but there were many injuries and debris from the blast was found 300 yards (275 metres) away. Twelve hours later, a second car bomb exploded outside Balfour House in Finchley, north London, at the headquarters of the Jewish

Philanthropic Organisation for Israel and the Middle East. Four young women in a car that was passing Balfour House at the time were extremely lucky to escape with their lives. The total damage caused by the two explosions was about £10 million.

Letters claiming responsibility for both bombs were received by Arabic newspapers and the Palestinian Liberation Organisation (PLO) from a previously unknown group calling itself Palestinian Resistance Jaffa Group Palestine. Both bomb vehicles had been sold through auctions and the Audi's previous owner remembered seeing the man who bought it. He gave a good description and the vehicle the suspect had been driving – a silver BMW 323i, but made to look like a BMW Alpina. By a process of elimination, the vehicle was traced and found to have belonged to Jawad Mahmoud Botmeh. Surveillance identified a co-conspirator, Samar Sami Alami. The conspirators were both Palestinians from affluent families. They had both obtained degrees at British universities – Alami in chemical engineering and Botmeh in electronic engineering.

On January 17, 1996, Jawad Botmeh, Samar Alami and others were arrested while a number of houses were searched. At 31 Montrose Court, SW7, an address used by Alami, firearms, ammunition and documents, including chemical formulae relating to explosives that would be of use to a terrorist group, were found. They were charged with conspiracy to cause explosions contrary to the Explosive Substances Act 1883.

Four months later, at a safety deposit facility in Acton, west London, the owners forced open a unit because the period of hire had expired. They uncovered a terrorists' arsenal. Among the items recovered were firearms, ammunition, books on guerrilla warfare and a book entitled *Engineering Book of Explosives*, containing details of making and using all types of explosives, detonators and weaponry. A large quantity

of an explosive called triacetone triperoxide (TATP) was found, together with two viable improvised explosive devices containing TATP, totalling 6 kg (13 lb). These devices only needed a power source to be connected for them to be capable of detonation. The fingerprints of Alami and Botmeh were found on numerous items within the secure unit. TATP is an extremely unstable, dangerous explosive, commonly used in the Middle East. This was the first time it had been found in the UK. An order for these chemicals had been placed at a manufacturer in Birmingham, and had been signed for by a G. Davis. The same signature was used when the vehicles used to carry the bombs were bought at auction. At Samar Alami's home detectives found an application letter to the Popular Front for the Liberation of Palestine (PFLP) stating she was prepared to undergo military training.

During their 11-week trial at the Central Criminal Court, Samar Alami admitted that she had made TATP and that she had rented the storage unit. Both Alami and Botmeh admitted making the two viable devices found there. Botmeh admitted his involvement in the purchase of the Audi that had exploded outside the Israeli Embassy, but both denied any direct involvement in the bombing of the Israeli Embassy or Balfour House. They claimed that the bombs they had made, including the materials and books they had collected, had been for experimental purposes only. They told the jury that their intention had been to send the technology to the Occupied Territories in order for the Palestinian people to defend themselves against the Israelis. The prosecution was able to show that the real purpose of their actions had been to disrupt the Middle East Peace process.

In mitigation the defence counsel, Michael Mansfield QC, claimed that the bombs were intended to be only 'symbolic explosions against symbolic targets' and had been timed to go off when they would

Above British officers visit a memorial to NYPD officers in Battery Park, Manhattan, near the site of the World Trade Centre in New York following the 9/11 attacks.

cause limited injuries. This was rejected by the trial judge, Mr Justice Garland, who said to the defendants, 'Why you did it we shall perhaps never know, but on the evidence it didn't advance the Palestinian cause in this country or in Western Europe.' On December 16, 1996, Jawad Botmeh and Samar Alami were sentenced to 20 years' imprisonment and were recommended for deportation on their release.

Ten years earlier the Metropolitan Police and the Security Service uncovered a plot to blow up an Israeli passenger airliner travelling from Heathrow Airport. On April 17, 1996 an attempt was made to place a timed improvised explosive device, concealed in passenger luggage, aboard an El Al plane with 375 passengers and crew. The device would have detonated while the aircraft flew over Austria at 39,000 feet (12,000 metres).

A Jordanian, Nezar Hindawi, had concealed the device in the luggage of his pregnant girlfriend, Anne Murphy – an Irish national who was completely unaware of her boyfriend's background or the attack he was planning, which would have killed both her and their unborn child. When she boarded the plane Miss Murphy thought she was to travel to Israel, then

Jordan, to marry Hindawi. Hindawi was acting in concert with members of Syrian intelligence, who had provided him with the bomb and flown him to England disguised as a crew member of Syrian Arab Airlines. His attempt to leave London in similar disguise was thwarted by the discovery of the device and Hindawi was taken to a Syrian safe house where attempts were made to alter his appearance.

Following Hindawi's arrest and conviction, the British government broke off diplomatic relations with Syria and the Syrian Ambassador, together with members of his staff, were expelled from the UK. Hindawi's sentence of 45 years' imprisonment remains the longest imposed in the UK for a single offence and merits an entry in the *Guinness Book of Records*.

Terrorism overseas

The 9/11 attacks claimed the largest number of British lives ever in a single terrorist incident: 67 Britons died. The Met launched Operation Exchange which helped to co-ordinate the UK response. A team of MPS officers, along with others from regional forces, travelled to New York where they assisted the New York Police Department and FBI to identify victims. They also provided support to families and friends of British victims.

Since the attacks in New York and Washington, co-operation between the world's law enforcement agencies and specialist anti-terrorism units has been taken to a new level with an even greater exchange of knowledge and intelligence. The Anti-Terrorist Branch runs training courses in the UK and in other countries to help international law enforcement agencies improve their ability to investigate terrorist attacks. The Metropolitan Police also receives specific requests for help from overseas governments and international organisations. In the past five years, Met officers have travelled to Kosovo to investigate war crimes and

around the globe to assist in terrorist inquiries in such places as Bali, the USA, Pakistan, Australia and across Europe.

As a result of atrocities committed against Kosovan Albanian civilians between June 1998 and June 1999, the United Nations, under the guidance of the International Criminal Tribunal for the former Yugoslavia (ICTY), requested that the UK and other countries send teams to assist in the investigation. The UK team was led and substantially staffed by officers from the Anti-Terrorist Branch, assisted by the Metropolitan Police Photographic Branch and members of the then RUC, South Yorkshire, Avon and Somerset, Devon and Cornwall, Hampshire and Greater Manchester Police. The first Anti-Terrorist Branch officers arrived in Kosovo only four days after the UN committed ground forces, forcing the withdrawal of Serbian army and police units into the former Yugoslavia. The British forensic team was the first into Kosovo and the last to leave. They exhumed in excess of 500 bodies, including those of 49 women and 19 children. Their equipment all had to be transported from the UK and organised from New Scotland Yard, including food, water, forensic equipment and other logistical support.

The investigation into the Bali bombings represented

Above A building in the Kuta beach area of Bali goes up in flames after one of a series of bombs was detonated outside a nightclub frequented by Western tourists in October 2002; 202 were killed in this terrorist atrocity. Met detectives flew to Bali to help with the inquiry.

an international response to a devastating terrorist attack on tourists and travellers who had come from all over the world. The sophistication of the attack and the huge number of casualties represented a significant challenge to the diverse group of police officers involved in the inquiry.

On October 12, 2002, at approximately 11.08 p.m. local time, three improvised devices were detonated in Bali, Indonesia. The first explosion was in Paddy's Bar in Kuta – a popular nightlife venue for young Australians and other Western tourists. The explosion occurred on the ground floor of the building, causing a large flash fire which ignited small spot fires inside the bar. The impact of the blast caused immediate death and injuries at the seat of the explosion. About 15 seconds after the bomb exploded at Paddy's bar, another large device exploded outside the nearby Sari Club. The bomb had been left in a white van and the sound of the blast was heard up to 9 miles (15 km) away. Less than a minute after the second explosion, a third, smaller device detonated. It had been placed 165 yards (150 metres) away from the American Consulate in Renon.

The explosions in Kuta killed 202 people and injured 168, many seriously. Of the dead victims, 25 were British, 88 Australian, 34 Indonesian and the remainder originated from other parts the world. Apart from the appalling loss of life, the blasts destroyed 422 buildings. At the invitation of the Indonesian government, a joint investigative team was established between the Indonesian National Police (INP) and the Australian Federal Police (AFP). The INP retained the lead role in the investigation but assistance was welcomed from other law enforcement agencies, including the Metropolitan Police Anti-Terrorist Branch. Within 24 hours of the bombings, a team of Met detectives flew to Bali. As the scale of the attacks became apparent, further British officers were sent to Bali to assist. These originated from throughout the UK and included family liaison officers, body recovery teams and victim identification officers. In the UK, at the request of the Foreign and Commonwealth Office, the Metropolitan Police Central Casualty Bureau opened and processed missing person reports from concerned relatives and friends.

The Anti-Terrorist Branch established an incident room to co-ordinate the investigation process in the UK. Witnesses who had returned to Britain were interviewed, and statements and other evidence which were obtained were passed on to the joint investigation team. These included exhibits, DNA samples, dental records. and lifestyle statements obtained from relatives of those who had lost their lives in Bali. Following a huge international investigation, a total of 33 trials took place in relation to the Bali attacks. Prison sentences imposed ranged from three years to life, and three defendants were sentenced to death.

A new threat on a new scale

Towards the end of the last millennium the Metropolitan Police and Security Service had severely limited PIRA's ability to mount campaigns in London and the rest of the UK. Thirty years of running operations both on the mainland and in Ireland meant that officers knew the enemy well. They understood how PIRA operated – like a military machine, with quartermasters, finance people, security teams and reconnaissance teams. They also knew where people stood in the hierarchy.

The attacks on the USA on September 11, 2001 established a new threat and a challenge to counter-terrorism on a scale that hitherto had been unimaginable. There is no negotiable political outcome with Al-Qaeda and its allied groups. No notice is given of the terrorists' attacks and their specific intention is frequently to inflict mass civilian casualties. The terrorists readily deploy the tactic of suicide attack – a concept alien to PIRA. Al-Qaeda operatives often regard such attacks as 'martyrdom operations'.

Another major difference is the method of attack. With PIRA the weapons of choice were the bullet and the bomb. It is feared that Al-Qaeda are prepared to use chemical, biological, radiological and nuclear (CBRN) devices, as well as military hardware such as air-defence missiles, and will countenance spectacular and simultaneous attacks such as those that occurred in the USA, Madrid, Morocco and Turkey. Officers who have worked on cases involving the worst atrocities committed by the IRA are appalled at the prospect that international terrorists are willing to detonate a radioactive device or 'dirty bomb'.

The size of the policing challenge has had a huge impact on resources. Since 9/11 the number of Metropolitan officers engaged in terrorist policing has grown considerably and will continue to do so in the

foreseeable future. The size of the Anti-Terrorist Branch alone has increased considerably and the other elements of the security services have also increased in size to counter the international threat. Those new staff will generate more intelligence, which will be passed to the Metropolitan Police and other police services to respond to.

The challenge now facing the Met and its law-enforcement allies is to gather high-quality intelligence about international terrorist groups. This challenge is far harder when the core of the group being targeted may be on a different continent. This means that the international effort and sharing of intelligence between countries has to be more sophisticated. Steady progress is being made on this front. Across Europe the level of co-operation between police and intelligence bodies has reached the stage where real-time sharing of information during a live operation against a terrorist group is possible. A few years ago such a concept would have been hard to imagine.

The objective of the Metropolitan Police Service is to make London a hostile environment for terrorists to attempt to work in. In order to do that, police need to target not just terrorist operational activity but all the things they need to do to support their existence. For example, extensive cheque and credit-card fraud is committed to fund these networks. Document and identity theft is another crime with a direct link to terrorism. The Anti-Terrorist Branch makes presentations to representatives of the retail industry, making it clear that terrorists rely on such criminality to fund their activities. With the new international threat, the traditional 'footprint' of a terrorist in an urban conurbation no longer applies. Recent anti-terrorist operations have involved forces from many counties and arrests have been made across the UK.

All the above now effectively means that the investigation of terrorism can no longer be viewed just as a specialist policing function. Every single Metropolitan officer and member of support staff has a role to play. There is also a need to engage a wider group of people who can enhance the security of London and the rest of the UK. Civil aviation security is one area of concern post-9/11. However, it is not just about preventing terrorists boarding an aircraft armed with guns or knives. There are many commercial airports and aerodromes in the UK and they vary greatly in size and use. The challenge is to have up-to-date intelligence about exactly who is using them and who owns the planes, as well as publicising the role that airport staff, security personnel and the general public have to play in the fight against terrorism.

Operation Rainbow

Since 9/11 the MPS has implemented a strategy to ensure that the global terrorist threat is met with proper synergy between the various organisations responsible for the capital's security. Operation Rainbow is a linked anti-terrorist strategy involving all of London's police forces (City of London and the British Transport Police, as well as the Met), the security services and other emergency service bodies. Rainbow also includes representatives from local government and the private sector – in short, any agency involved in reducing the threat of a significant terrorist incident in London.

Far left A Met officer wears a protective suit during a joint exercise with other emergency services designed to test London's response to a chemical or biological terrorist attack. Since 9/11 the Met has faced a huge policing challenge from the threat of international terrorism.

Left Public vigilance, as encouraged by this poster on the London Underground, remains vital.

Rainbow combines preventative work, proactive intelligence gathering, post-incident investigation and the accumulation of evidence. It gives the Met a menu of contingency plans and tactical options that cover a range of policing activities to respond to the ever-changing threat from terrorism.

Rainbow allows the Met the opportunity to work with the private sector to increase the security of London. This includes the training of private-sector security guards to enhance their awareness of the threat and train them how to provide an initial response to a bomb. It also ensures the consistency and efficiency of the Met's access to CCTV surveillance cameras. Operators are reminded to regularly change the tapes, store them safely and wipe the lenses on the cameras to ensure the quality of the footage.

Each week the Assistant Commissioner responsible for Specialist Operations, David Veness, chairs the Security Review Committee, which is attended by a number of people who, in effect, are the key operators responsible for providing London's security against attack. It also allows specialist departments within the Met, such as Special Branch, to come together with territorial commanders who provide the patrolling strength on the ground. A separate Rainbow meeting is held at borough level every two weeks to update PCs and sergeants in each area of the Met on what is required to enhance security. During each meeting the Committee reviews the week's events, possible threats and their impact on the police and other services. These range from arrests that are part of anti-terrorist branch operations, protests and marches involving political or religiously motivated groups, state visits and even international events that have an impact on UK security. The various options needed to meet that threat are discussed and decided on, and the appropriate level of security is agreed.

Engagement with the community is vital in the fight against terrorism. The Met has well-established lines of communication with community leaders and is committed to building on the partnerships that already exist. Assistant Commissioner Veness chairs regular meetings with the Muslim Safety Forum, as well as the Community Security Trust that deals with Israeli and Jewish issues.

London has been a target for acts of violence from Irish, international and domestic terrorists for well over a century and, as one of the world's major cultural and economic centres, it will continue to be a target for the foreseeable future. The Met has the unique experience of policing such a challenging environment. Indeed, the Met's delivery of counter-terrorism and security policing is 'the envy of the policing world', according to the first HMIC baseline assessment of the Metropolitan Police Service, 2004.

6　Technology and kit

The equipment carried and used by early Metropolitan Police officers was extremely basic – a deliberate policy designed to reassure the public that London's police were approachable citizens in uniform rather than a quasi-paramilitary force.

Inevitably, the spread of modern communications, faster modes of transport and information technology have forced the police to keep pace with such developments. But while the Met has always carefully assessed the operational suitability of each new piece of kit and the impact it would have on its public image, criminals have been under no such restraints.

The last 25 years, in particular, have seen policing develop into a high-tech battle to keep one step ahead of increasingly sophisticated and dangerous forms of criminality. This has sparked a revolution in the technology and kit carried and used by the Metropolitan Police. It has transformed uniforms, the protective equipment carried by officers, communications and intelligence methods, both open and covert. 'Going equipped' has long been a police term used for criminals who carry firearms, jemmies and other 'tools of the trade.' These days the Met are more than likely to be a match for whatever they are using.

Communication

Effective communications and reliable intelligence are the bedrock of modern policing, and 21st-century technology has revolutionised the speed and quantity of information that can be handled by the Metropolitan Police.

The Service has come a long way since its Victorian beginnings when the only means officers had to call for assistance were rattles and whistles. Today, global positioning systems guided by satellites allow Met control rooms to keep precise track of police vehicles and individual officers. The gulf in the technology may be huge but its purpose is the same – police officers have always needed a reliable means of communicating with colleagues and their stations.

One of the most iconic sights of 20th-century Britain was the Metropolitan Police box. These blue kiosks, with flashing lights on the roofs, were rendered obsolete by the introduction of personal radios in the 1960s. But they have been immortalised by the cult television series Dr Who, which depicted a London police box as a vehicle for time travel. The real thing was somewhat less spectacular, consisting of a telephone connected to the local police station that could be used by officers and members of the public in an emergency. Inside was a stool so that beat officers could eat their sandwiches without getting rained on.

Between 1966 and 1969 a radio system was rolled out across all Met divisions, allowing officers to stay mobile and keep in contact. Until comparatively recently police radios have been generally cumbersome and unreliable. Atmospheric conditions interfere with transmission and some areas become known as 'black spots' because geographical features or other factors render normal reception impossible. A new national police radio system, known as Airwave, is being introduced to tackle these problems. The new digital system will allow officers to access local and national databases, such as the Police National Computer (PNC). It also suppresses background sounds so officers can be heard in the noisiest places. The handsets can be used as radios, mobile phones or pagers, and all transmissions are encrypted to a very high level, which makes it very difficult for criminals to monitor police frequencies. The Airwave system is also being made available to other emergency services, such as paramedics, fire brigades and the coastguard. A compatible radio system across all emergency services would be a great asset when dealing with major incidents, such as rail crashes or terrorist attacks.

While it is essential that police officers can communicate with each other in a secure and effective way, it is equally important that the public can contact the police quickly and easily. London was the first area in the UK to introduce the number 999 for automatically telephoning the emergency services. In its first week, in 1937, the system received 1,300 calls. That figure has grown exponentially so that today the Met receives approximately forty to fifty thousand calls for emergency assistance from the public each week. The Met estimates that only 80 per cent of calls to this number are genuine emergencies. For example, people have used the number to ask advice about stain removers or kitchen plumbing problems. With this misuse of the 999 service, and the ever-increasing use of mobile phones, demands made on the Met's command and control systems are extremely high. The Service is now putting in place a major overhaul of these systems (see chapter eight) to increase the effectiveness of its response. Under the current system, borough-based control rooms act as call-handling centres for all emergency calls made within the Metropolitan Police District. They alert local officers and arrange the appropriate level of response if specialist back-up – such as an armed response vehicle

(ARV) or a hostage negotiation team – is needed. Housed within New Scotland Yard is the Special Operations Room known as GT, which is used to monitor and control major public-order operations such as demonstrations, festivals and ceremonial events. Its computer system keeps track of resources and a bank of television screens connected to key CCTV sites gives the gold commander a grandstand view of events from inside New Scotland Yard.

Another separate unit that performs a vital role in major incidents and disasters is the Casualty Bureau, which deals with enquiries from victims' relatives and friends. The Bureau was started during the Second World War air raids on London. It was realised before the war that in the event of casualties, details about those killed and injured would have to be circulated through local police stations. By 1940 Met officers were collecting lists of those killed and injured during German bombing from hospitals and mortuaries. Casualty lists would then be sent to divisional police stations by teleprinter, duplicated on special machines and circulated to the other stations within the division.

Above A London police woman demonstrates the new walkie-talkie radios introduced in 1965. Until recently police radios were generally cumbersome and unreliable.

Next of kin or other relatives would then be informed by police, if this had not already been done, and messages would be sent to provincial forces if relatives lived outside London. The heavy air raids on London in September 1940 produced casualty lists of such length that teleprinters could not cope and printed and typed lists had to be produced as well. By the end of November 1940 some 700 casualty lists, containing a total of more than 32,000 cases, had been circulated, and 1,872 messages had been sent to provincial police forces.

The modern Casualty Bureau system was developed following a train crash in Lewisham in 1957. Today, the Central Casualty Bureau (CCB) is a model of policing excellence that has been used to respond to incidents outside London and in other countries. Following the terrorist attack on New York's World Trade Centre in 2001, for example, the CCB opened to deal with calls from the relatives of British victims. Staff

received up to 1,000 telephone calls per hour immediately after that attack. Private and government organisations from all over the world have visited the CCB and training has been provided to police forces from as far away as Bermuda. The CCB is staffed by volunteers from across the MPS. Both police officers and police staff work together when CCB is opened. During an incident they need to be able to work in a highly pressurised environment, and as a consequence all staff undergo a week of intensive training and have regular refresher courses.

After a major incident the main tasks of CCB staff is to obtain and process relevant information about the people involved or potentially involved in the disaster. The Bureau also receives details of casualties and fatalities from police documentation teams at the scene, as well as from hospitals and mortuaries, and then matches survivor and missing person records and casualty and missing person records. The CCB provides a vital link by providing accurate information direct to relatives, the senior officer at the incident and the coroner. It also provides support to family liaison

officers who work closely with relatives of victims and investigation teams. The CCB recently relocated from New Scotland Yard to Hendon and has increased its pool of 200 staff to 300. The new facility has more capacity to receive calls – there are 80 per cent more call positions dedicated to dealing with public enquiries. It also has an uninterrupted power supply and generator at Hendon, as well as a fall-back facility at an alternative MPS site to ensure that vital support can be maintained in the event of a major disaster in central London such as a terrorist attack. CCB is also now using the best technology. Laptops increase mobility and can be used at any incident around the world, allowing a direct connection and relay of information to CCB via satellite link. This removes the need to rely on local resources and allows the Bureau to have direct access to an incident at any time, anywhere.

Electronic surveillance

In London alone, there are over 150,000 CCTV cameras, and it has been estimated that on average

UAITING
E HILL
5 13/04/02

Far left The Met's Casualty Bureau system for collating and disseminating information about victims following major incidents, has been copied around the world. It has proved vital following incidents such as the Paddington rail disaster.

Left Fighting football hooligans are captured on CCTV footage in April 2002. Evidence provided by CCTV footage has proved crucial in a number of high profile investigations.

every person is captured on film at least eight times every day.

Installation of CCTV began in the 1970s, though its widespread use only started in the 1990s. Some of the systems are controlled and operated by the Met, some are council run and many are installed by factories, car parks, businesses and retail outlets. Together these systems provide a powerful surveillance network that covers almost every street in London. Evidence provided by CCTV footage has proved crucial in a number of high-profile investigations, including the murder of Jill Dando and the hunt for nail bomber David Copeland (see chapter four).

Modern surveillance systems involve a linked series of cameras, with full pan, tilt and zoom functions, capable of remote operation from a control room. Picture clarity can be excellent, with many systems capable of zooming in to provide a clear image of an object the size of a cigarette packet from 100 metres away. Other cameras are less sophisticated and if poorly maintained can render the images they produce of little or no evidential value. With the increased threat of terrorist attacks since 9/11, CCTV is a crucial cog in the machinery that monitors London's security. With this is mind, the Anti-Terrorist Branch has mounted a campaign to ensure systems are properly set up and maintained. Operators are encouraged to change the tapes in the cameras on a daily basis and use them no more than 12 times to maintain picture quality. It is also crucial that the time and date displays are correct and the footage produced is clear enough to identify people and vehicles. Some CCTV system operators have stepped up a level and installed sophisticated software that enables the cameras to produce intelligence about crime.

The London Borough of Newham became the first local authority to add a digital face-recognition system to its CCTV network. This works by taking live pictures from the camera and downloading them to a computer, where a program checks the faces shown on camera and compares them against a database of active local criminals. The same identification technology is also being used to automatically recognise vehicles that have been involved in crimes. Automatic Number Plate Recognition (ANPR) systems check up to 3,000 number plates per hour and can take readings on vehicles travelling up to 100 m.p.h. (160 k.p.h.). Number plates are then checked against a variety of databases, including the PNC, DVLA and local intelligence databases.

When it was first tested in London in 2002, ANPR helped the Met to seize £14,700 in illegal drugs, and recover 28 stolen vehicles and £9,500 in stolen goods over a nine-month period. Trawls using ANPR can be extremely effective in tracking cross-border criminals – the so-called 'level 2' category of offender. A recent ANPR trawl resulted in the arrest of a man wanted in connection with murder investigations. A search of his home address resulted in the seizure of substantial quantities of drugs, and officers also came across body armour and passports. The Met now uses ANPR Intercept Teams to conduct

Above Computer systems inside modern police vehicles provide officers with access to a range of information, including criminal records and global positioning systems.

intelligence-led policing operations, targeting priority crimes such as street robbery and gun crime. It has been estimated that ANPR could result in the MPS making 3,000 more crime arrests in London every year.

Transport

The Metropolitan Police has been set a target of arriving at the scene of all 'immediate response' incidents within 12 minutes of a 999 call being made. Given the number of incidents that require such a response, the size of London and the volume of its traffic, achieving this target is no mean feat. The scale of the task could not have been envisaged by Sir Robert Peel, whose concept of a professional police service was based on highly visible foot patrols.

The Met did not acquire its first car until 1903, when a Vauxhall Cabriolet was purchased for the Commissioner's use. Although the Flying Squad acquired pursuit vehicles after it was established in 1919, the first widespread motorised patrols did not start until 1930. Today the Met is in possession of a comprehensive fleet of vehicles designed for general patrol, fast response and firearms duties. Prototype armoured vehicles were introduced at Heathrow Airport last year as a counter-measure against the threat of terrorist attacks.

Public concern over the number of accidents involving police vehicles has led to tight control over the way officers respond to emergency calls in vehicles or pursue suspect vehicles. The decision on whether a police vehicle should remain involved in the pursuit of another vehicle rests largely not with the driver but in a police control room. From this central point, officers can take an objective view of the incident. Traffic, road and weather conditions, as well as information and intelligence on the target vehicle and the driver, may

Above Three Eurocopter AS 355N 'Twin Squirrel' police helicopters stationed at Lippitts Hill, north-east London provide officers with an 'eye in the sky' 24 hours a day.

change rapidly over the course of a pursuit. The job of the control room is to take a continual risk assessment of the incident as it develops and to make decisions on the tactics required to bring it to a safe conclusion. This may involve ordering the police vehicle to stop its pursuit of the target vehicle, if necessary.

An alternative to using road vehicles for such incidents is provided by the Met's Air Support Unit (ASU). Three Eurocopter AS 355N 'Twin Squirrel' helicopters operate from the ASU base in Lippitts Hill in north-east London providing air support for Met officers. An aircraft is on standby 24 hours a day. Primarily, the helicopters are used at major events to monitor and direct crowds and to provide an extra element of security. But the ASU is a pan-London resource, and every Met officer can call for air support in the same way they would ask for armed back-up or other specialist assistance. Around 60 per cent of the unit's time is devoted to spontaneous response in areas such as suspect and vehicle searches, but the

helicopters can also be used for preplanning and proactive operations. A nose-mounted camera in the helicopter contains a TV camera, linked to control rooms, and thermal imaging equipment that allows the crew to see people and vehicles on the ground even in the dark. A powerful searchlight also allows search operations to be conducted at night. The unit produces aerial photographs and images, or video footage, to assist in briefings and operations, and the helicopters can also be used for proactive, intelligence-led patrols.

Protecting an unarmed service

London's police service is one of the only metropolitan law enforcement organisations in the world that, to a large extent, performs its role without the routine carrying of firearms. In fact, for the majority of its 175-year history, the protective equipment carried by most Met officers remained basically the same – a wooden truncheon. The lack of weaponry carried by the majority of officers was not an oversight but deliberate policy. Robert Peel's template of a civilian service that would not appear to the local community as an army of occupation has helped establish a unique level of trust between London's police service and the community it

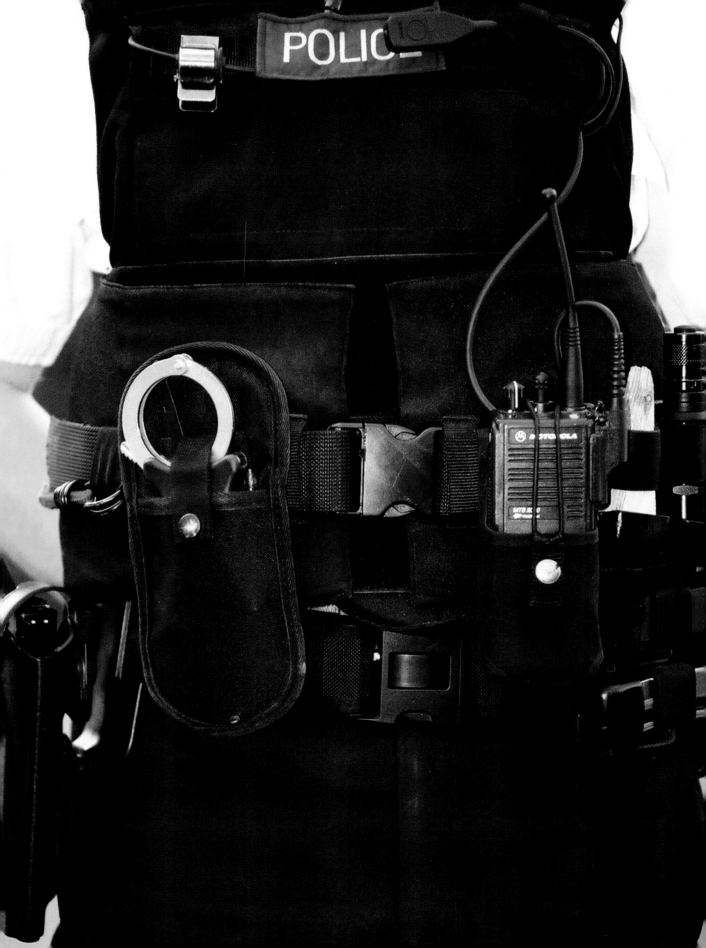

protects. But this trust has sometimes come at a price for the men and women who wear the uniform. Over two centuries, routine acts of outstanding bravery by Met officers have led to hundreds of commendations, serious injuries and loss of life. The Met's Roll of Honour appears at the back of this book.

Until the 1990s, the only standard protection officers had against attacks was their own negotiating skills and, if that failed, a 15-inch (38 cm) crocus-wood truncheon with a leather thong handle. This was issued to all uniformed constables, sergeants and inspectors and kept in a special pocket in the uniform trousers. CID officers were issued with a slightly shorter version, while the Mounted Branch was given 36-inch (91 cm) batons, which were carried on the horses' saddles.

While the increase in armed crime is of growing concern to Met management, the biggest threat to London police officers has always been attacks with edged weapons. This threat of knife assault was what prompted a revolution in police protective equipment in the 1990s. Longer batons, CS spray and personal-issue body armour provide officers with better protection and the ability to fend off or incapacitate an attacker without resorting to routine arming. In 1994, following extensive trials of four different types of baton, a 22-inch (59 cm) acrylic version was introduced to be worn on the uniform belt. More recently this was replaced by a 'gravity friction lock' baton that is collapsible, making it less clumsy for officers to wear.

CS sprays were introduced in 1997 as standard equipment for patrolling officers. The small propellant canister spray can deliver a directed jet of CS into the face of an attacker. It causes extreme irritation to the eyes, nose and throat and in the majority of cases will stop an attacker in his tracks, allowing the officer to make a controlled arrest. There are strict guidelines for the use of CS – it should never be used indiscriminately against a group or in a confined space, for example. The third element of new equipment gives officers protection against gun and knife attack. There is no such thing as a 'bullet-proof' vest as there are certain types of ammunition that can penetrate most types of body armour. But the MetVest, which is issued to all frontline officers in London, comes as close to that concept as current technology will allow.

Body armour that can protect against both knife and firearm attack is hard to design without being too heavy or bulky for officers to wear throughout an eight-hour shift. But the MetVest offers a degree of protection against both forms of attack and is light enough to be worn for regular police duties. The original Metvest, introduced in 1997, was an innovative piece of protective equipment at the time but was not comfortable for women officers because of their different physical shape. After consultation with officers, the Met drew up a new specification that recognised the need for a lighter-weight product with additional sizes and flexibility of design. The MetVest2 offers the same protection level, is lighter and is more flexible.

There is no doubt that the new equipment has changed the look of London's police officers on the streets. It could be argued that the packed equipment belts and body armour worn by most officers suggest a more paramilitary style of policing. An equally strong argument is that 21st-century London police equipment is a triumph of compromise, which recognises the threat from a more violent society but sticks to the tradition of unarmed policing.

Left The introduction of body armour and other protective equipment such as CS spray and batons has increased the safety but changed the look of London's police officers.

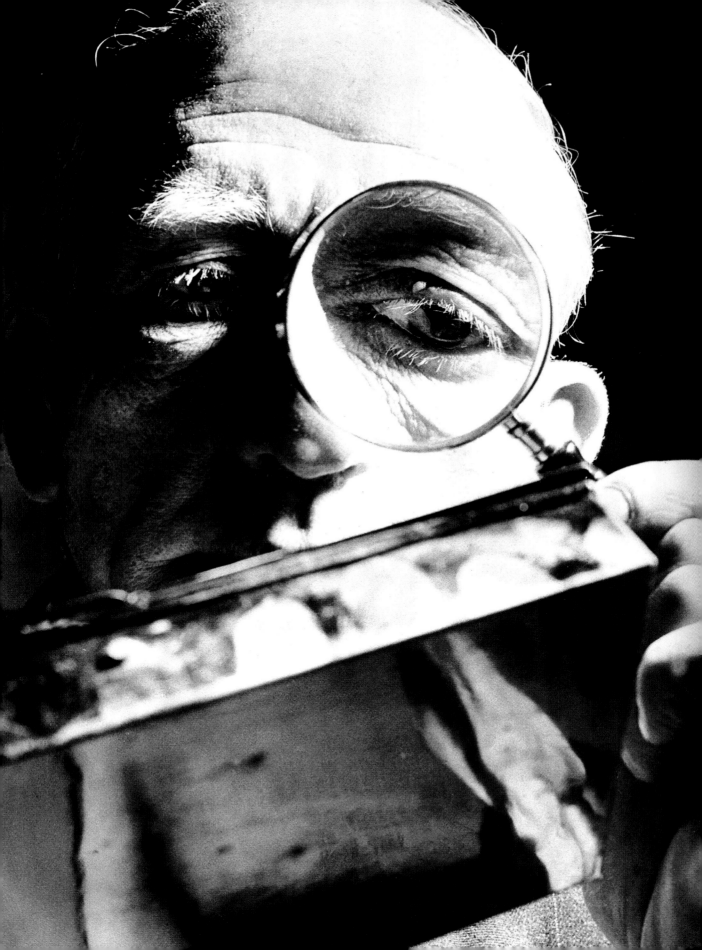

7 Forensics

It is a testament to the reliability of fingerprint evidence that today it remains the principal method of identification in criminal cases. While the principles of the 19th-century technique remain the same, the early fingerprinting pioneers could not have envisaged how advances in technology would transform their art. Refinements to the system and computerisation have revolutionised the speed of identifications and the number of 'hits' that can be achieved.

This quantum leap has been reflected in other areas of forensics that today are proving to be crucial investigative tools for the Metropolitan Police Service. The development of modern techniques such as DNA profiling, for example, has allowed detectives to re-investigate and solve crimes which are decades old.

Throughout its long history, this innovative and constantly evolving area of work has continued to help the Met meet its most difficult challenges.

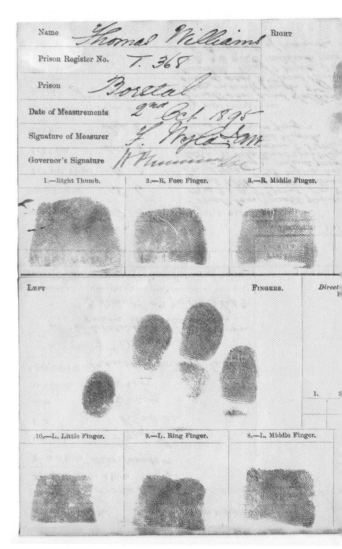

Fingerprinting

Although fingerprints had been used in India since the early 19th century in proof and disproof of identity, no reliable system to search for and file fingerprints among thousands of others had existed in the UK until Edward Henry, a member of the Indian Civil Service, developed one. Henry published his book describing the system, *Classification and Uses of Fingerprints*, in 1900.

As Inspector General of the Bengal Police, Edward Henry found himself in charge of a force that, in 1892, adopted the French anthropometrical identification system. Initially Henry favoured this system but later began to question the accuracy of such measurements. At the beginning of 1897, with assistance from two of his most able staff, he introduced an identification system based purely on fingerprints. By the summer of that year the 'Henry' system of identification had been introduced in all of British India.

Fingerprint identification was based on the discovery that the papillary ridges on the skin surface of each finger, the palm of the hand and the sole and toe of the foot are unique to each individual. A person's fingerprints develop during the third and fourth months of foetal life and persist throughout a lifetime without change (unless through deep-seated injury). They are also one of the last things to decompose after death.

The skin's ridge system is dispersed irregularly with ridges that fork and ridges that end abruptly. The points at which these occur within the ridge system are referred to in fingerprinting parlance as 'ridge characteristics'. Identification of prints is conclusively established when it can be shown that a sufficient number of their characteristics match and relate to each other perfectly and no characteristics are found to be in disagreement with one another other The case for two people having the same fingerprints has never been proved. Every individual bears a unique set of 10

different fingerprints; even identical twins have unique and different finger and palm prints.

The Henry system of classification enabled the fingerprints of an individual to be easily indexed, searched and filed among thousands of others. Such a system was of vital importance to the police because it effectively prevented professional criminals from concealing their criminal records by changing their appearance or giving a false identity on arrest.

In July 1900, a five-man Home Office committee chaired by Lord Belper sat to consider the merits of 'Identification of Criminals by Measurements and Fingerprints'. So profound an impression did the evidence of Edward Henry make on the committee that their subsequent report, published the following November, stated, 'The advantage of fingerprints as a means of proving identity is no

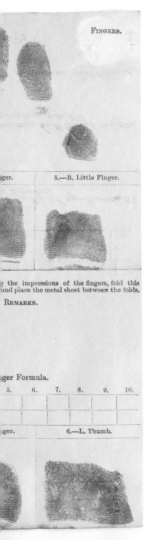

Left An example of an early criminal record identification card held at Scotland Yard (1895).

Above The genius of Sir Edward Henry's identification system, introduced in 1901, lay in the classification of records. An English Heritage plaque was unveiled in 2001 at Sir Edward's former London residence in Sheffield Terrace, Kensington.

longer open to discussion.'

Henry, having returned from a recent posting to South Africa, joined the Metropolitan Police as Assistant Commissioner in March 1901, and four months later, on July 1, established the first fingerprint bureau in the United Kingdom at Scotland Yard. His system was used for the first time to convict burglar Harry Jackson in 1902. It also proved its worth in establishing the criminal credentials of the numerous pickpockets who were arrested each year at the Epsom racecourse on Derby day. These petty thieves often gave the police false identities and claimed it was their first offence. In 1902 two-thirds of those arrested were shown to have previous convictions.

By the end of that year the Fingerprint Bureau had confirmed the identities of more than 1,700 habitual criminals. It was perhaps fitting that a few years later

the value of fingerprints as a definitive means of identification in a murder case was demonstrated for the first time in this country at the Old Bailey.

The Deptford murder case

Alfred and Albert Stratton were a pair of professional thieves from Deptford who, in the process of robbing a local oil and paint shop in 1905, killed Thomas Farrow, the owner of the shop, and his wife Ann. Although the police suspected the Stratton brothers during the early part of their investigation, witnesses who had seen two men running away from the scene were unable to identify them.

However, when Detective Inspector Collins of the Yard's Fingerprint Bureau examined a cash box discovered on the floor beside the bed of the murdered Ann Farrow he found a thumb mark left by Alfred Stratton. This led to both men being charged and brought to trial. The trial was interesting in that it marked a clash between the new science of fingerprinting and the older technique of anthropometrics.

A former member of Scotland Yard's Anthropometrical Department, Dr John G. Garson, was hired as an expert witness by the defence counsel to discredit the fingerprint evidence. Despite this attempt to undermine the prosecution, the jury, having listened to expert witness Detective Inspector Collins from the Met's Fingerprint Bureau describe the fingerprint identification process, quickly returned a guilty verdict on the evidence of the thumb mark, and the men were found guilty and hanged.

The Stratton case proved that fingerprint experts who work in the Metropolitan Police carry a heavy weight of responsibility to ensure that the identifications they establish from tiny finger and palm marks found at crime scenes are accurately arrived at.

Fingerprint evidence as proof of identification

In 1909 the Criminal Appeal Court ruled that a judge or jury could accept fingerprint evidence on its own as proof of identification. Herbert Castleton had been convicted on the sole evidence of a finger mark on a candle found at a crime scene. Castleton's lawyers appealed. The judge asked them, 'Can the prisoner find anybody whose fingerprints are exactly like his?' No, was the answer. The Appeal Court upheld the conviction.

Since the 1950s the role of a fingerprint officer has largely been civilianised in the Metropolitan Police, but it is just as specialised as CID or firearms officers' duties. It takes at least three years' training to qualify as a fingerprint expert and between five and ten years to become a senior expert, qualified to deal with homicide and terrorism cases.

Until recently the Fingerprint Bureau had to prove that there were at least 16 identical characteristics between a mark found at a crime scene and a fingerprint record in order for that to be presented in court as positive identification. This numerical minimum has now been removed and each individual fingerprint expert determines identification. However, it is an established national procedure within the UK to

have an identification checked independently by three separate officers, two of whom must be at least of expert level, before confirmation of identification is released to the authorities. In some cases four checks are performed. More recently, 'Third Level Detail' – the use of pores, creases and even permanent scarring – has been used in identifications in more serious crimes.

Before fingerprint records were computerised, it could take days to match a crime-scene mark. In 1984 an Automatic Fingerprint Recognition (AFR) system was introduced in the Fingerprint Bureau to speed up the process. AFR uses digital matching techniques and high-accuracy algorithms to match scene-of-crime marks against a fingerprint database. The Met has kept pace with advances in fingerprinting technology and was one of the first UK police services to sign up to the National Automated Fingerprint Identification System (NAFIS) in 1998. This has allowed the Service to make upwards of 10,000 positive identifications each year – more than five times as many as Henry's system was able to achieve.

But the expertise does not just rely on making an accurate identification that will be acceptable in a court of law. The job of searching for finger and palm

Far left Scotland Yard's Fingerprint Branch, circa 1925. Before fingerprint records were computerised it could take days to match a crime scene mark. Now the service can make 10,000 positive identifications each year - more than five times as many as Henry's system.

Near left Scenes of Crime Officers (SOCOs) were first recruited in 1969, and are trained to retrieve all types of forensic and other physical evidence, including finger marks. In the future, technology may allow SOCOs to make identifications at crime scenes rather than in the laboratory.

marks at crime scenes and then 'lifting' or photographing them so that they can be analysed is just as specialised.

Scenes of crime officers

Scenes of crime officers (SOCOs) were first recruited by the Met in 1969 in a bid to augment the relatively small elite field force of District fingerprint experts and to increase the number of crime-scene examinations conducted each year. These officers were trained to retrieve all types of forensic and other physical evidence, including finger marks.

The most common method involves 'dusting' a surface with fingerprint powder and lifting any finger and palm marks that may develop with adhesive tape. The tape bearing the marks is then transferred on to small stiff sheets of plastic, thereby preserving the mark(s) from any damage and corruption. These 'lifts' can then be presented as prosecution exhibits at trials. Finger, palm and foot marks that are left in malleable surfaces such as mud, wet paint or putty can be photographed rather than dusted. Certain exhibits, such as paper retrieved from crime scenes, may undergo sequential chemical treatment in search of finger and palm marks. Examinations by alternate light sources

are now commonly used, not only in searches for finger and palm marks but also to discover other forensic clues, such as blood and semen. Cyanoacrylate fuming is another commonly used method to develop finger and palm marks.

Vacuum metal deposition is a development technique that is especially effective on non-porous surfaces, like plastic or latex, which do not respond well to powder or other chemicals. This technique was used successfully more than 20 years ago to identify the men involved in the shooting of a Metropolitan Police constable.

PC Philip Olds was shot during an armed robbery at an off-licence in Hayes, Middlesex two days before Christmas in 1980. He had gone into the shop to buy cigarettes, only to be confronted by two armed men wearing balaclavas who had just robbed the shop. PC Olds drew his truncheon and attempted to arrest the men, one of who opened fire. A dumdum bullet fired by the robber severed PC Olds' spine, causing instant and permanent paralysis from the chest down.

Fingerprint experts completed a detailed examination of the scene and obtained numerous finger and palm marks which could have belonged to any one of the thousands of customers who had visited the shop. The breakthrough came when a white plastic carrier bag found lying on the counter of the shop was submitted for examination by means of vacuum metal deposition. It was believed that the bag had been used by one of the armed robbers to conceal the handgun used to shoot PC Olds. Finger marks were developed on the bag, which were photographed and scanned onto the AFR system for search against the Yard Fingerprint Bureau's database of millions of fingerprints. Within 15 minutes they were identified as belonging to the left thumb, forefinger and mid-finger of Leslie John Cooke. Cooke was convicted of attempted armed robbery and attempted murder. His accomplice Stuart Blackstock was convicted of wounding with attempt to resist arrest and received a life sentence.

The same fingerprinting technique was used to solve the death by arson of seven members of the same family in March 1999. This was an example of an excellent 'cold' search result on a barely searchable mark. Four generations of the family died when the family home in north-east London was set ablaze on March 6, 1999 after someone poured petrol through their letterbox. The ages of the victims ranged from two to 76, and included three-year-old twin girls and a boy of two.

Left PC Philip Olds was paralysed when he was shot during a robbery at an off-licence in 1980. Finger marks found on a plastic bag used by the criminals to carry the gun later secured their conviction for attempted murder.

A red plastic petrol can was found close to the scene and was preserved for fingerprint examination, which was carried out at the Serious Crime Unit. A poor-quality mark was developed by the vacuum metal deposition method. Photographs of the mark were brought to the Fingerprint Bureau and a search carried out using the automatic fingerprint recognition (AFR) system.

The system provided more than a hundred possible matches for the mark. By calling up each fingerprint record and examining them individually, a fingerprint expert was able to identify a match on the 55th sample identified by the computer. At his trial Richard Fielding pleaded guilty to the crime on the grounds of diminished responsibility, and is currently being detained under the Mental Health Act on seven counts of manslaughter.

The Knightsbridge safe deposit robbery

Fingerprint evidence also played a crucial part in solving what was possibly the largest robbery that has ever taken place in the UK. It is estimated that around £40 million was stolen in cash and other valuables from deposit boxes held at a centre in west London, but this is only an estimate as many of the owners of the boxes have not come forward to declare their losses.

In his autobiography, Valerio Viccei claims that the real figure was closer to £60 million. Viccei was an international criminal who had been jailed in his native country of Italy for terrorist attacks. He graduated from politically motivated crimes to armed robberies because of personal greed, and after a series of bank robberies in London he decided that the Knightsbridge Safe Deposit Centre would be next.

On July 12, 1987, two men visited the centre on the pretext of renting safe-deposit boxes. While being shown around, they produced firearms and overpowered the manager and security guards. A notice was placed

Left The Knightsbridge safe deposit robbery in July 1987 netted thieves at least £40 million in cash and valuables. Although the gang wore gloves to avoid detection, the leader cut his finger in his haste to open the boxes and left a blood stained print that led to his conviction.

on the front door apologising to customers and explaining that the centre would reopen the next day. With the help of more men, who were let into the vault, the thieves broke open the boxes with power drills, sledgehammers and crowbars. Viccei and the rest of the gang had been careful to wear gloves during the raid, but in his eagerness to open the boxes Viccei made a fatal error which was to lead to his arrest and conviction. He had torn his glove and cut his finger. An hour after the thieves left one of the handcuffed captives freed himself and raised the alarm.

Several days were spent collecting evidence, and although many finger marks were found, one set created particular interest. On the inside of the deposit-box door numbered 2722 were a number of finger marks, but one of them in particular caught the eye of the fingerprint experts examining the scene. The mark had been made in blood. Fingerprint officers began a search through the national fingerprint collection of 4.5 million sets of prints and a match was made. The prints were identified as belonging to Viccei, whose prints had been circulated by Interpol in connection with a string of armed robberies on the Continent.

The Metropolitan Police Flying Squad traced Viccei and put him under surveillance. He was eventually arrested while driving around London in his Ferrari. Viccei was convicted along with several others and in 1993 was transferred to an Italian jail to await trial for offences in that country. He was later shot dead by the Mafia. The manager of the centre proved to be a member of the gang and he, too, was convicted for his involvement in the robbery.

Terrorism and forensic evidence

Fingerprint and other forensic evidence has proved crucial in the successful prosecution of terrorists. Thorough crime scene examination and the development of more advanced techniques for retrieving finger and palm marks have helped detectives pull off the policing equivalent of finding a needle in a haystack following terrorist attacks. The latest developments in photography and digital imagery have also advanced the capture of crime scene marks and has allowed for the removal of background interference on items such as bank notes.

After a bomb has gone off it is unlikely that crime scene officers are going to find a detonator in the wreckage marked with a terrorist's fingerprints. It was also unlikely that experienced Provisional IRA active service units would use people whose fingerprints were already held on police records. But other material gathered from the scene or elsewhere, which could be linked to terrorist suspects once they were in police custody, was often recovered through forensic and fingerprint examination. This has allowed Anti-Terrorist Branch officers to link the suspect with more than one attack.

A classic example of this was the extensive fingerprinting work that led to the conviction of the Docklands bomber responsible for ending the PIRA ceasefire in February 1996 (see chapter five). Evidence retrieved near the scene of the bomb allowed Met officers to identify the lorry used to transport the bomb. Tachograph recordings and CCTV surveillance footage were used to track its movements from Northern Ireland through to Scotland and onwards to London. They were also able to establish that the driver of the lorry had stayed at a truck-stop hotel in Carlisle on the journey south.

Met fingerprint experts examined four rooms at the hotel. Among items taken for forensic examination was a glass ashtray. The team also retrieved a number of other articles, including a trucking magazine and a number of ferry tickets for a return journey between Belfast and Stranraer. Among the latent marks developed on these items were three impressions of the same right thumb. The quality of the mark developed on the ashtray was such that a search of the national fingerprint database could be undertaken. More than 350,000 responses were viewed on NAFIS, with a negative result. The thumb print was also searched by the Scottish Criminal Records Office and the RUC's Fingerprint Bureau, also with negative results.

The following year RUC officers arrested a PIRA active service unit in South Armagh, Northern Ireland. Their fingerprints were taken to the RUC fingerprint bureau where the latent thumb mark on the glass ashtray was identified as belonging to one of the suspects. He was flown to London and fingerprinted. Further comparison work revealed that a total of 14 marks from the Met operation were identical with the suspect's fingerprints. These included marks on the ferry tickets, the truck-stop registration form for the room where the glass ashtray was found, the lorry park ticket and the trucking magazine, which had been bought in the Irish Republic. The suspect was later charged with the Docklands bombing.

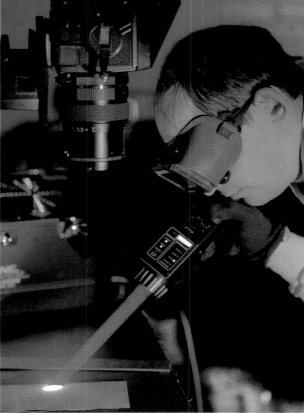

Far left The Metropolitan Police opened its Forensic Science Laboratory in 1935 in recognition of the crucial role forensic techniques play in investigations.

Near left Techniques using lasers, light sources and chemicals have been developed to enhance the finger and palm marks left at a scene.

Forensics as an investigative science

Major crime scenes such as that facing the Metropolitan Police after the Docklands bombing are essentially jigsaw puzzles, where the accumulation of forensic evidence demands a variety of techniques to fit the pieces together. Since 1935, when the Metropolitan Police opened its Forensic Science Laboratory, science has remained at the cutting edge of police work.

Increasingly sophisticated methods have been developed for examining blood and semen stains and in the identification of explosives and ballistics. The laboratory also examines alcohol and drug levels in blood or urine samples, as well as the type and purity of substances seized during drug operations. Analysis of handwriting and other documents have provided decisive prosecution evidence in a number of cases. A technique using electro-static detection apparatus (ESDA) can reveal impressions of handwriting made on a sequence of folios on a pad or other writing material. Not only has this revealed important information in fraud and terrorism cases, it has also provided vital evidence in incidents of police malpractice where witness statements or entries in officers' notebooks have been altered.

The Serious Crime Unit was formed in 1984 to increase the yield of forensic evidence gathered from the scenes of murders, rapes and terrorist attacks. The unit consists of a multi-disciplined team of fingerprint experts, photographers, biologists and chemists. Techniques using lasers, light sources and chemicals have been developed to enhance the finger and palm marks left at a scene. This technique was used on a knife recovered from a robbery scene. A very small fragment of a fingerprint mark – about 4 mm in size – was found on a rivet on the handle. Although this comprised only four or five 'ridges', lasers were used to enhance the mark and a positive match was made against a suspect's fingerprints. Members of the unit have also become experts at isolating and identifying flecks of paint, fibres and other material that may provide vital clues.

Today the Met's fingerprint and forensic staff are an integral part of tackling crime in London. They carry out 11,000 scene examinations every month and generate 14,000 identifications of suspects. This contribution spans the whole range of crime from simple thefts from motor vehicles to terrorism offences.

Demands for forensic services in police work continue to grow. The high-profile miscarriages of justice that came to light in the late 1980s, which led to a Royal Commission on Criminal Justice in 1993, changed the way prosecution evidence was viewed in the courts. Evidence obtained by police officers through interviews, or indeed their own observations was no longer sufficient to sway juries. Scientific evidence gathered at the scene, which was incontrovertible, took on a vital significance.

The importance of scene examination following terrorist attacks (see chapter five) and in murder cases (see chapter four) has taken those demands to a new level. Forensic searches at scenes now often take in a wider area and therefore take more time. If, for example, someone is murdered in a London park today, it is more than likely that the entire park will be sealed off so that a forensic examination of the whole area can be undertaken. Ten years ago that would not have happened. It represents a large commitment of resources in return for a statistically small chance of success, but in difficult cases it can provide a breakthrough.

The DNA breakthrough

The development of DNA profiling by Dr Alec Jeffreys at Leicestershire University in 1986 was hailed at the time as the most important development in forensic science since the introduction of fingerprint identification at the turn of the 19th century. It has allowed crime scene examiners to retrieve traces of body tissue or fluid, including blood, semen, hair or bone that can positively identify both victims and suspects. The sensitivity of the technique has developed at such a pace that it has become possible to obtain accurate DNA profiles from increasingly small samples. Since Dr Jeffrey's discovery there have been five generations of DNA profiling techniques – each one more sensitive and discriminating than the last. With the earliest techniques, a blood stain the size of a 10p coin was needed. It is now possible to obtain a profile from a pinprick of blood or a hair root.

DNA has given senior investigating officers an

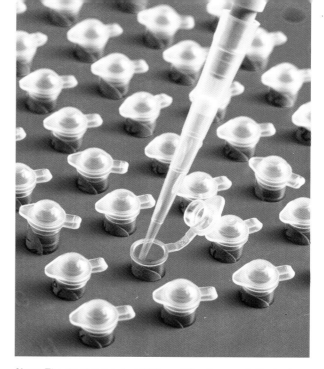

Above The development of DNA profiling has revolutionised police investigations. It is now possible to obtain a profile from a pinprick of blood or a hair root.

important new tool to enable them to identify suspects and provide powerful evidence that will lead to a conviction in a court of law. Yet fingerprinting is still the primary forensic technique used by the Met and other police forces, and the establishment of DNA testing has certainly not made the use of fingerprints any less important. At crime scenes, for example, there will often be DNA evidence in circumstances where there are no fingerprints, and vice versa.

Violetta Vella, 83, was murdered at her flat on a north London estate on February 18, 2002. The victim's daughter had been trying to contact her mother by telephone all day and, concerned that there was no answer, she went to the flat and let herself in using her own set of keys. Although there was no sign of her mother inside the flat, cupboards and drawers had been disturbed. She later found her mother's body under a pile of clothing at the foot of the stairs.

Stab wounds had been inflicted to the victim's throat and her clothing had been disturbed. On a bed in one of the bedrooms, scenes of crime officers found a blue sweatshirt, which did not fit in with the other items of clothing found in the flat. On closer inspection it was found that blood was visible on the sweatshirt and it was submitted to the Forensic Science Service for DNA testing.

On March 1, 2002, a profile obtained from the sweatshirt resulted in a 'hit' on the national DNA database for Rodney Anyanwu, who had not been previously associated with the inquiry. Various items of the suspect's clothing were submitted for examination, and blood from the victim was located on a pair of trainers. In a knife block in the kitchen of the flat, crime-scene examiners had found a blood-stained knife. The blood matched that of the victim, while a DNA sample taken from the handle of the knife indicated that all DNA components matching Anyanwu's profile were present.

Approximately 200 finger or palm marks were identified inside, or on items removed from, the victim's flat, but incredibly none of them matched Anyanwu's. The DNA evidence, on its own, was enough to convince a jury of Rodney Anywanyu's responsibility for killing Violetta Vella, and he was detained without limitation for time under the Mental Health Act.

Sometimes combinations of different types of forensic evidence will provide positive identification of a suspect. It may be, for example, that an individual mark or sample retrieved from a crime scene provides a partial match, but when combined with other forensic evidence it helps to build up a powerful prosecution case.

Jackie Martyn-Box was a retired professional woman who lived alone in a first-floor flat in Surbiton. She started using a local minicab company for transport after she had a road accident and her car was taken off the road. On February 22, 2001 a neighbour, who had let herself in, found her lying dead on her hallway floor with a cut to her throat. The flat appeared undisturbed and there were no signs of forced entry. A post-mortem revealed severe internal injuries to the chest, as well as broken ribs.

At an early stage in the investigation Glen Galley, a South African national, who had been working as a local minicab driver, came under suspicion. Police enquiries revealed that Galley had befriended the victim, often borrowing money from her. As a result of the scene examination, Galley's fingerprints were found in the hallway of the flat and his shoe prints in the soft mud in the communal gardens that surrounded the block where the victim lived.

Galley was staying at the YMCA in Surbiton. Officers searched the building and found jewellery concealed in the washroom at the hostel. During interviews Galley stated he had been to the victim's address some weeks previously, but on the night of the murder he had been at the cinema with his girlfriend. He told officers that the jewellery found in the washroom belonged to a former girlfriend who was living back in South Africa.

DNA tests were carried out on the jewellery and a partial match was made with the victim's DNA and on samples of jewellery found in the flat. The shoe marks found in soft mud in the communal gardens were also used as evidence, although they had been mixed in with the shoe marks of the building's caretaker, who had used the path on the morning the victim's body was found. These two pieces of evidence, combined with the finger marks found inside the flat, played a big part in the successful prosecution for murder. Galley received a life sentence.

Operation Sapphire

Rape remains one of the most under-reported of all crimes and research suggests that as few as one in ten victims report the crime to the police. In addition, conviction rates have been falling for a number of years while public confidence in the criminal justice system has been declining. The Metropolitan Police recognised the importance of addressing these issues and, following extensive consultation both inside and outside the police service, Project Sapphire was started in January 2001.

Sapphire is dedicated to improving victim care and the investigation of rape. At the outset a detailed action plan was drawn up setting out the most comprehensive reform programme on the investigation of rape that the Met had ever undertaken. As a result, more victims have had the confidence to report rape and more offenders have been charged with this horrendous crime.

Overall, the operation is achieving a higher clear-up rate in rape cases; figures for 2002/3 show that 124 more cases of rape were cleared up compared to the previous year and 25 per cent of rapes reported to the Met resulted in a charge. In the same year, the Met recorded a more than nine per cent increase in the number of victims reporting this crime to the police. This is a direct result of more victims coming forward to report rapes because of increased confidence and trust in the Met. While excellent progress has been made, there is still much work to be done and Sapphire remains committed to further improvements.

One such step has been the introduction of dedicated sexual assault referral centres. Known as 'Havens', these centres have been opened in Camberwell in south-east London, and Paddington and Whitechapel in west and east London respectively. The Haven centres are a major development in the improvement of victim care and the Metropolitan Police has established a ground-breaking partnership with the NHS to fund them at a cost of £1 million each. The introduction of the centres means that rape examination suites in police stations, which were often intimidating environments for victims, are no longer used.

Victims are brought to the centre in unmarked police cars by specially trained police officers. Only one victim is in the centre at any time to ensure quiet and privacy. Victims are seen by specially trained medical professionals, who offer comprehensive medical care in purpose-built facilities. The medical staff also gather the forensic evidence that is so vital to police investigations and successful prosecutions. These services are available to victims by reporting to the police or, just as importantly, access can be gained independently of the police.

Sapphire cold case investigations
Another recent innovation has been the introduction of a Sapphire Cold Case Investigation Team. Advances in forensic science and scene examination have allowed the Metropolitan Police to revisit old cases and apply new techniques not available at the time to try and solve so-called 'cold' cases. Although much of the media focus of cold-case work has been on high-profile homicides, the Service feels that the technique has an equally vital role to play in the re-investigation of rapes and child abuse inquiries. Although some of these cases may be ten or 15 years old, there is a high possibility that the person who committed the crime remains 'active', given the re-offending rate among sexual offenders.

The Sapphire team has begun reinvestigating more than 1,500 unsolved stranger rape cases dating back to 1987. It is the biggest review exercise ever undertaken by a single police service. The cold case reviews have been made possible by improvements in forensic analysis which mean that forensic samples retrieved at the time of the offences can now be examined for minute quantities of DNA. Samples taken from old evidence can then be profiled and compared with the records held on the national DNA database. The potential for clearing up unsolved cases is huge, and Sapphire detectives are optimistic that a one in three success rate might be achievable.

Cold case rape investigations are extremely sensitive inquiries and officers have to be conscious that victims may be re-traumatised by a fresh investigation into a crime they have tried to put to the back of their minds.

Left The National Fingerprint Identification System (NAFIS) holds 5.5 million sets of prints. Electronic imaging machines in custody suites allow the Met to take a suspect's prints electronically and will substantially increase the number of records held.

The victims will be a lot older and may not have told their present partners about the rape. They may well have moved to different areas, changed their names or even emigrated. In cases where fresh evidence has emerged, officers conduct careful research into the background of both the suspect and the victim before deciding how to proceed with the inquiry. Despite these difficulties, Operation Sapphire has achieved some notable convictions.

In January 2004 officers and forensic staff working on the operation's cold-case team secured a landmark conviction for a rape committed in 1989. Carl Junior Fridye, 32, was convicted despite the fact that the witness never gave a statement and died before the case went to court. Fridye broke into the 77-year-old's ground-floor flat in her Holloway sheltered accommodation and sexually assaulted her as she lay in bed. Local CID officers began an investigation and the victim was medically examined, but she was too traumatised to make a full written statement to police. The work of the cold case team and advances in DNA techniques meant forensic scientists were able to re-test and identify previously unidentified

samples of Fridye's semen on the victim's sheets.

Once Fridye's profile was determined and his fingerprints resubmitted, he was searched in the national database. This led to his arrest in Birmingham. Using the Metropolitan Police intranet, the Sapphire team launched an appeal for information from officers who had worked on the original investigation 14 years previously. By talking to these officers and backtracking through paperwork, the Met was able to build a prosecution case, but it took 10 months. This painstaking and thorough investigation culminated in the conviction of Fridye.

Cyber-SOCOs – the future of forensics

London has always had a large transient criminal population. This was true even before Sir Robert Peel's Act established the UK's first professional police service 175 years ago.

Sir Edward Henry introduced his fingerprint identification system at the turn of the 20th century to prevent repeat offenders from disguising their criminal backgrounds. The problem for the Metropolitan Police in the modern era is that the

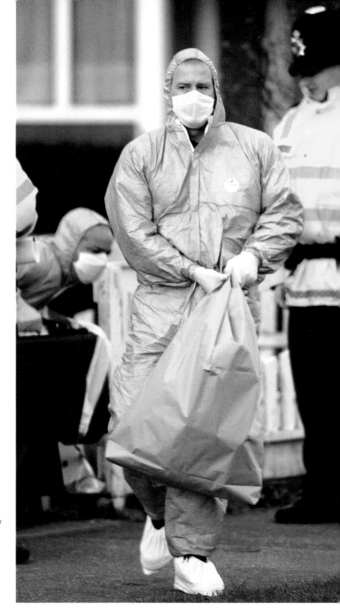

population of London has become a lot bigger. There are now approximately 44,000 people wanted for criminal offences within the Metropolitan Police District. Many of these individuals are wanted for serious offences such as murder, rape, robbery, aggravated burglary and serious assault.

As policing in the capital moves into the 21st century, that challenge remains the same but the demand for identifications is greater. Politicians, the public and even police officers expect quicker results and increasingly look to forensic science to help them achieve those results. An average of 800 people are arrested and processed through Metropolitan Police cells every 24 hours. Many come into police custody on suspicion of committing relatively minor crimes, but there is a high probability that a proportion of these may be wanted for more serious offences, but manage to evade detection by giving officers false details and are therefore released on bail.

In this respect, it could be argued that the greatest breakthrough in forensic science over the past 30 years has not been DNA profiling but the development of 'intelligent' computer databases that can store millions of identification marks – whether they be fingerprints or DNA profiles. The national DNA database now holds just under 2 million suspect/offender profiles. It also holds 180,000 DNA profiles from stains found at scenes of crime. The National Fingerprint Identification System (NAFIS) holds 5.5 million sets of prints.

From 2004 a change in the law has allowed the Met to take fingerprints and DNA samples from suspects who have been arrested for a recordable offence. The change in legislation means that an estimated 60,000 extra samples will be added to the databases every year. Electronic imaging facilities in custody suites – known as Livescan units – allow the Met to take a suspect's prints (finger and palm) electronically. The units are linked to the national fingerprint database so that the police are able to confirm a person's identity in a matter of minutes. DNA samples taken in connection with routine offences will give the Met an opportunity to conduct a cold search of the national DNA database for a corresponding crime scene stain in a more serious case.

This has shifted the whole emphasis of how forensic science is used by the police and the demand for forensic work in general. DNA, fingerprinting and other techniques are now used as much to develop criminal intelligence as provide evidence of a crime in court. Increasingly, forensics is being used by the Met to solve volume crime such as street robbery and burglary. In 2003, for example, there were significant increases in the number of scenes examined and crimes solved through forensics. Forensic intelligence is being developed to support the implementation of the National Intelligence Model. This will link crimes such as burglary and robbery through fingerprints, DNA and footwear.

The potential for using DNA to solve volume crime such as street robbery and burglary is yet to be fully explored, although submission levels for the Service are now among the highest in the world. In the 12 months from April 2002 to 2003 more than 10,000 crime samples were submitted for DNA profiling, including almost 5,000 for burglary.

DNA profiles have been generated from over 50 per cent of the samples submitted and almost 6,000 crimes have been linked to suspects through the DNA database. The Met has created the role of DNA Development Manager to maximise the use of DNA evidence and keep up to date with advances in technology. The manager acts as a consultant to units such as Operation Sapphire.

Metafor, a major new IT system, will manage all the Met's forensic information from 2005. A major part of its introduction will see crime scene examiners using mobile devices to record crime scene information and input it directly into Met computer systems. The system will track exhibits and cases from 'cradle to grave' by using mobile devices at crime scenes.

The National Automated Fingerprint Identification System (NAFIS) can search marks and fingerprints from all 43 police forces in England and Wales. Its replacement, the IDENT1 system, will develop, in addition to fingerprints, a national automated palm print identification system. Palm prints can be recovered from around

20 per cent of crime scenes, and in about six per cent of cases they are the only marks that are recovered.

Despite advances in technology, it is still quicker to obtain a result from a search for fingerprints than it is to wait for DNA results to be available. Even from a good sample, it takes, on average, 48 hours to get the result of a DNA profile, whereas a search of the fingerprint database can produce a match in minutes. This is set to change. Developments in bio-chip technology could enable a new generation of 'cyber-SOCOs' to conduct a DNA profile at the crime scene. This does not just increase the speed of the search. Because the scene examiner will be more aware of the significance of what they have found than someone back at the laboratory, they will be able to provide a more effective service to the senior investigating officer (SIO) in charge of the case.

After DNA, what will be the next breakthrough in forensic science? Having perfected a method for analysing body fluids, the next major development could be the analysis of body odours. As it has been proved that tracker dogs can follow an individual and identify them by smell, can that natural process be simulated via some sort of electronic nose? Analysis of smell is currently used as a diagnostic tool in the food industry and in medicine where, for example, diabetes can be diagnosed by the smell of a patient's breath. Dutch police have already used analysis of a suspect's body smell in a court case.

Historically, most major developments in forensics have been by-products of research in other areas. DNA profiling is a prime example as it was developed from medical research into genetics. Hand-held DNA devices, or bio-chips that could be used at crime scenes may be developed initially through US research on the detection of biological agents used on the battlefield during germ warfare.

8 The future

What would Sir Robert Peel make of today's Metropolitan Police Service? In many ways it has changed beyond all comparison. In terms of size, the number of officers in London has grown from a little over 1,000 to more than 30,000. The geographical area covered by the Met is now some 625 square miles compared to the seven-mile radius from Charing Cross that was envisaged in 1829.

Peel established his police service to tackle violent criminality and although murderous assaults were a common problem in early Victorian London, it could not have been imagined that 175 years later there would be a sustained threat to the capital from international terrorists determined to inflict mass casualties.

Peel's force would also have had no experience of meeting the challenge of 'volume crime' such as burglary, robbery and vehicle crime that London officers have been attempting to tackle since the Second World War. The pressure that volume crime has put on the Met's resources has been huge and by necessity has revolutionised the way that policing services are delivered.

Above Community policing is still the bedrock of the modern police service according to Commissioner Sir John Stevens.

Organised crime

The challenge posed by organised crime has also undergone a paradigm shift in a few decades. It has been estimated by the National Criminal Intelligence Service (NCIS) that 70 per cent of all organised crime in the UK is based in London.

In response to the emergence of organised immigration crime, the Metropolitan Police has set up a specific operation in partnership with the UK Immigration Service and the UK Passport Service. Operation Maxim was launched in April 2003 and targets gangs involved in serious criminal activity. This includes kidnapping, drug trafficking, human trafficking and money laundering. Operation Maxim also targets those individuals who exploit vulnerable members of emerging communities in London. It is spearheaded by the Met's intelligence section, SCD11 (Specialist Crime Directorate), based at New Scotland Yard, which has formed a joint intelligence cell with the Immigration Service. The scale and capabilities of such joint operations will be strengthened by the formation of a new national agency to tackle organised crime.

The creation of the Serious Organised Crime Agency (SOCA), announced in February 2004, will see the merger of the National Crime Squad, National Criminal Intelligence Service and the investigative branches of Customs and Excise and the Immigration Service. The aim of the new agency will be to enable intelligence and operations to combine in a seamless approach. In this way it will enhance the sharing of intelligence, resources and experience across all the agencies involved, and harness this power to strengthen the prevention and detection of crime. SOCA's primary target will be crime that significantly impacts on the UK and is co-ordinated by criminal organisations across the nation and between countries. It is expected to be operational by 2006.

The significance of London in organised crime coupled with the expertise housed within the Met's Specialist Crime Directorate will ensure that the MPS remains at the heart of the UK's policing response to all new and sophisticated forms of criminality. The Met's recognition of the policing skills at its disposal through the training provided by the Crime Academy (see chapter four) represents an investment for the future.

Community policing

Today London is a teeming city of some seven million people and 29 per cent of the city's population belong to minority ethnic groups. More than 300 languages are spoken.

Despite the vast differences in scale, many of the roles of the Metropolitan Police have changed little since Peel's time. The Service is still tasked with delivering locally-based policing by consent, reducing crime and the fear of crime, and maintaining the security of those who live and work in London. Over the last 175 years there have been huge advances in technology, communications, transport and forensic science, yet the Met recognises that locally-based, neighbourhood policing is what concerns the majority of Londoners.

Under the 'Safer Neighbourhoods' initiative, designated teams made up of a minimum of a sergeant, two police constables and three Police Community Support Officers (PCSOs) tackle local 'quality of life' crimes such as graffiti, vandalism and general forms of anti-social behaviour. The Met has reopened 15 small local police stations within the last five years, which had been closed under the old area command system, and has plans to open more.

Community policing has always suffered from the problem of 'abstraction', where local officers are removed from their areas to provide aid in other parts of London, mainly for public order situations such as demonstrations, marches or major sporting events. Under the new system, the Safer Neighbourhoods teams are safe-guarded, ensuring that every neighbourhood or ward in London will eventually have its own permanently designated police team.

It may surprise some people to know that the current Commissioner, Sir John Stevens, recognises the potential of the bobby on the beat as a thoroughly effective modern crime fighter. Sir John cites the example of Lewisham PC, Clifford Cutts, who was awarded an MBE after walking the same beat for seven years in one of the toughest parts of London. He has been stabbed twice and has had objects thrown at him from the estate walkways he passes under every day. But he is known and respected by the local community and has also helped to reduce crime significantly in his area.

In Peel's day London was still a major port and there was a certain amount of smuggling and organised crime, but it was mostly localised. The complex nature of the threat today and the demands it places on the Metropolitan Police are massive. The Met is now called upon to deliver a response to the challenges of international terrorism and organised crime that is way beyond anything that might have been envisaged when

Sir Robert Peel established the Metropolitan Police. At the same time, it also has to provide a policing service to London in a locally and fully accountable way. Both are equal priorities.

There have long been debates within policing circles about the nature of local and cross-border crime and the link between the two. Sometimes the two problems can be seen as competing concerns, but Sir John says the Met cannot deal with each in isolation and an integrated response is essential. 'Of course we have got to deal with organised crime and terrorism. Specialist officers such as those in the Flying Squad or who work on Operation Trident have achieved major successes, but the bedrock of policing hasn't changed in 175 years. It is out there on the street, walking, dealing with things and communicating with local people. Some of our best terrorist successes have been based on information from local officers', he said.

Only neighbourhood-based policing can deliver a local service, and after the 9/11 attacks in the USA, 1,000 officers were brought in from the outer London boroughs to deal with the threat of terrorism in the centre of London. However, there is a significant local policing element to even large-scale terrorist operations.

The Service is under no illusion about the threat to London posed by an attack by Al-Qaeda or one of its associated groups. However, Sir John Stevens says, 'The knowledge and experience built up over 30 years of dealing with the mainland campaign mounted by the Provisional IRA (PIRA) has been invaluable. The Metropolitan Police and the security services have built the most successful counter-terrorism partnership in terms of arrest and convictions that the world has ever seen.'

Given the threat of terrorism and the criminal use of firearms, the delivery of a largely unarmed policing

service in London should not be taken for granted. In a recent incident a police personnel carrier was sprayed with machine-gun fire. Fortunately, none of the officers present were seriously hurt. The number of armed officers has increased significantly over the last two years - to cope with both the increase in gun crime and to provide added security. But the current Commissioner is a firm believer in the unarmed police officer continuing to provide the bedrock of local policing, and he is keen for the Met to hold on to that tradition for as long as it possibly can. Certainly, a significant number of serving police officers have indicated a desire to maintain their unarmed status. This situation can only be maintained if there is adequate armed back-up available and the number of armed officers is reviewed on a weekly basis.

With over 30,000 officers and 12,000 support staff, the Met is a very large organisation, bigger, for example, than the Royal Navy. Occasionally, local and national politicians will suggest that it is too big to deliver the kind of local service that people want, but the Commissioner argues that London is a region with its own political and cultural identity and should retain a police service that reflects that.

Resources

The biggest problem the Met has had to face in the modern era has been dwindling resources. When Sir Paul Condon became Commissioner of the Met in 1993 he had 28,500 officers under his command. Seven years later that figure had dropped to a little over 25,000, even though the population of London had grown by a million people and the demands on the organisation had increased significantly.

A fourfold increase in emergency 999 calls and the new threats posed by international terrorism resulted in a major campaign by the Met's leaders to convince their political masters that London needed more police

Above and above right The number of specialist officers has greatly increased in recent years. The number of recruits has also increased to cope with the demands of policing such a large city as London.

officers. The success of this can be measured by the fact that all the major political parties have now signed up to having 35,000 sworn officers on the streets of London. That is in addition to the 1,500 PCSOs who are already on patrol and the further 1,000 that the Service hopes to recruit.

This marks a sea change in the organisation. Five years ago the Met could only recruit 60 police officers a month. Because of wastage rates and other factors, if that level of recruitment had continued the Commissioner believes the Metropolitan Police would have 'disappeared into the sand'. Now 60 people a day want to join and the Met has had to suspend taking applications in order to clear the backlog. Surveys have shown that some 68 per cent of Londoners say they are prepared to pay more towards policing provided they see those police officers on the street. In 2003 the Met hit the milestone figure of 30,000 police officers – the highest in the organisation's history and is now working towards the target of 35,000. The moves to extend the Met 'police

family' have also been ground-breaking, with the introduction of PCSOs in 2002. Without full powers of arrest, but with the authority to detain suspects for up to half an hour, they have been extremely well received by the public and have freed up highly trained and experienced police officers to deal with crime. The Met has also recruited 170 detention officers to replace uniformed staff in dealing with suspects who come into police custody.

The unique office of police constable has altered little since Robert Peel's time. It carries with it powers and responsibilities that represent an affirmation of public faith and trust in the ability of police officers to protect and act on their behalf in order to maintain law and order. Sir John is keen to ensure that this extended police family does not lead to the erosion of that status and the powers that go with it. 'I am a firm believer in the office of constable. It's a unique position that enshrines the operational independence of the person wearing the uniform. Any erosion or damage of the status of a constable will betray 175 years of policing impartiality. Let's not throw the blue uniform and the helmet away. They have a powerful symbolic importance that is based on respect.'

As part of the modernisation of the police service,

the issue of whether officers should be employees instead of state appointees has been put under the spotlight and the debate continues as to whether the normal range of benefits, working conditions and sanctions that apply to other professions would be effective for the police service. Employment issues aside, there are several aspects of the police regulations that many regard as draconian and old-fashioned. The police disciplinary system is viewed by the Met's management as a relic from the 19th century, with procedures that are akin to a military court martial for dealing with routine employment problems. Because pay and other conditions of service are negotiated on a national basis, the Met has not been able to place a premium rate on being a police officer in London. Local bargaining and paying what the market demands to attract the best applicants would give management more flexibility.

And while the Met may be going back to its roots with its focus on local neighbourhood policing, it is looking to deliver it in a thoroughly modern way. The 'C3i' project represents a huge investment in the way the Met communicates with the people of London and responds to calls for assistance. The revolutionary command, control, communication and information

Above Commissioner Sir John Stevens and the Deputy Commissioner, Sir Ian Blair, attend a Metropolitan Police Authority (MPA) meeting.

programme will enable the Service to deal more effectively with the growing number of calls it receives. It will also provide frontline officers with a range of new communication technology such as hand-held computers and other mobile data devices.

Phone calls received from the public and the appropriate response from the Met will be managed from three new state-of-the-art centres in London at Hendon, Bow and Lambeth. Borough operations rooms, open around the clock, will distribute fast-time local intelligence and safety instructions to frontline officers, and in-car computers will provide direct access to the

Police National Computer, mapping systems and other criminal intelligence databases.

C3i represents a technical revolution in the way the Met delivers its services, and is one of the biggest changes in the way the police are deployed across the capital that the Met has undertaken in the last 175 years.

One of the legacies of Peel's new police was the fact that the Met Commissioner was made directly accountable to the Home Secretary. Until 2000 the Met was the only police service in the UK that did not have its own police authority. Now, it could be argued that the Met has more layers of public scrutiny and accountability than any police service in the country. The London Mayor sets the budget and the Metropolitan Police Authority (MPA) establishes policing priorities and monitors the Met's performance. The establishment of the MPA marked a fundamental change in the policing of London. It is an independent statutory body, established under The Greater London Authority Act 1999, and came into effect in July 2000.

The Authority gives Londoners a regime of local democratic accountability for policing that previously did not exist – its duties and responsibilities formerly rested directly with the Home Secretary. Members of the Authority scrutinise and support the work of the MPS. The Authority's Community Engagement Committee holds public meetings every two months to find out Londoners' concerns about policing in the boroughs and crime and community safety in general. Members of the Authority also have regular contact with community groups and individuals in the boroughs. The MPA Board is made up of 23 members, 12 from the London Assembly (including the Deputy Mayor) appointed by the Mayor, four magistrates selected by the Greater London Magistrates Courts Authority and seven independents, one appointed directly by the Home Secretary – the other vacancies are advertised openly.

'The Met is a very large and complex organisation and what we are trying to do is promote accountability at a series of different levels,' said former and founding MPA Chair, Lord Harris. 'There is force-wide accountability which we bring through our police authority meetings and our London-wide community work. We are also promoting and enhancing accountability at a more local level through borough commanders and crime and disorder reduction partnerships. We need to make sure that they are responding effectively to what the public think is important in their areas. Even more locally, at neighbourhood level, we are actively engaged in looking at ways in which we can enhance accountability and engagement with the community.'

Although the Home Secretary no longer acts as the police authority for the Met, the importance of the Service in a number of national policing functions means that it comes under closer scrutiny from central government than many other UK policing organisations.

Diversity

A major priority for the MPA and the MPS is to ensure that the Service reflects the diversity of London. Both the Scarman Report and the Stephen Lawrence Inquiry

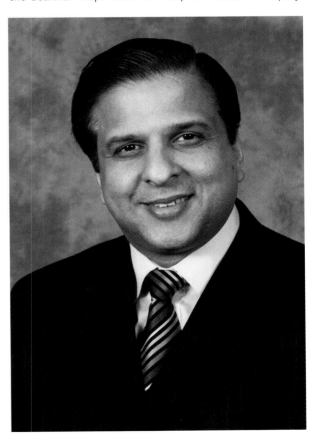

Above Tarique Ghaffur became the UK's highest ranking ethnic minority officer in 2001 when he achieved the rank of Assistant Commissioner.

highlighted the fundamental importance of community confidence and trust – and the need to build a police service that is truly representative of the population it serves.

Historically, a career in the Metropolitan Police Service might not have been a traditional choice for individuals from ethnic minority backgrounds, but this has changed dramatically in recent years. The percentage of police applicants from ethnic minority backgrounds is now rising steadily. The government has set the Met an ambitious target of having 25.9 per cent of its workforce from an ethnic minority background by 2009. Despite unprecedented success in ethnic minority recruitment, which has been supported rigorously both from within and outside the Service, it seems unlikely that it will be possible to achieve this without changes to existing race equality legislation.

Three years ago people from an ethnic minority background made up less than four per cent of the Met's workforce. The current figure is 6.6 per cent. While this is a big step in the right direction, the Service still has some way to go. In the year 2003/4 the Met recruited 3,400 officers, with approximately 15 per cent of these coming from minority ethnic groups. The evident success of the Met's recruitment initiatives to attract potential police officers from ethnic minority backgrounds is underpinning the Service's drive to become increasingly representative of London's community.

Lord Harris accepts that the target of 25.9 per cent by 2009 was a very challenging one. In summing up his personal view, he said, 'There is no question that it is an extremely ambitious target but it represents a proper direction for the organisation. The Met should broadly reflect the face of London. It is interesting that if you look at the mix of recruitment for Police Community Support Officers, it is much more reflective of London –

a third come from ethnic minorities and there is a much higher proportion of women. Another important point is that these are predominantly Londoners and I think that we should continue to focus on that.

'Whether we will achieve the overall ethnic recruitment target will depend on a number of factors. It is certainly my view that we need to have greater flexibility under the legislation to take much more explicit positive action to achieve the target. We also need to look at what other opportunities there are in terms of recruiting directly into the Met to ensure that we make real progress.' Lord Harris believes that this would involve, where appropriate, recruiting ethnic minority officers directly into specialist posts.

The law does not allow any organisation to discriminate positively in that way, but Martin Tiplady, the Met's Director of Human Resources, is interested in exploring how the Service could adopt processes to increase ethnic minority representation – but this would depend on legal changes being made. The thinking behind such a policy is that if the Met can fast-track sufficient numbers so that, for example, 12 per cent of the Met's officers are from ethnic minority backgrounds, it will be easier to build on that as a base.

Respect for diversity is not purely focused on race. The Met is committed to supporting any individual who considers the Service as a potential career choice. This support is provided regardless of age, religion, faith and sexual orientation or preference. Members of the Service who discriminate against their colleagues are not tolerated and a number of new internal initiatives have been developed to enforce this. There are now 13 staff associations in the Metropolitan Police representing different minority or national groups. They include the Disabled Staff Association, the Black Police Association, the Met branch of the British Association of Women Police, the Lesbian and Gay

Police Association and groups representing Christian, Muslim, Sikh, Hindu, Catholic, Jewish, Italian, Turkish, and Greek and Turkish Cypriot officers. The Met feels these staff associations send out a positive message about the diversity of the organisation and encourage recruitment and retention of officers from every background. They give advice on a range of issues affecting ethnic minority officers internally as well as advising on minority communities in general. They also provide support for officers seeking promotion within the organisation, and those with a grievance.

The number of women officers joining the organisation has also risen. Of the 3,400 people recruited during the last year, 1,000 were women. The proportion of female officers is now more than 18 per cent and the Met is confident that it will meet the target figure of 25 per cent by 2009. An increase in flexible working patterns, career breaks and the introduction of school-term working patterns are designed to help it meet that target.

The Positive Action Central Team (PACT) was created to address the desire to recruit more ethnic minority and women officers by promoting a career within the police to these groups. PACT aims to achieve its goals using a five-strand action plan, delivered across a series of pan-London and individual borough events and initiatives, as well as through the Met Careers Office.

The Metropolitan Police has come a long way in 175 years. When it was established in 1829 there was heated public debate about whether the new organisation would become 'an engine for despotism'. Such fears have proved unfounded. The scale of its task may have increased beyond all measure, but today London's police service is more accountable than it has ever been and engaged with its community to a degree that would have been unimaginable in Peel's time.

Above Commissioner Sir John Stevens is flanked by Prime Minister Tony Blair and London Mayor Ken Livingstone at the 2004 celebrations to mark the 175th anniversary of the MPS.

Roll of Honour

1924
PC Arthur Owen Holdaway Died of injuries received in 1923 when knocked down by a tram while on duty in Camberwell.

1927
Sgt Leonard Carter While checking insecure premises in Pall Mall he fell 35 feet down a shaft and was killed.

PC Percy Edwin Cook Killed by fumes as he tried to rescue two men collapsed in an inspection chamber at Notting Hill.

1928
PC Raymond Cyril Mitchell Fatally injured when struck by a motor cycle combination while on point duty at Wallington.

1929
PC David Fleming Ford Killed when he fell through a glass roof while pursuing burglars across rooftops at Lambeth.

PC John Arthur Self Fatally injured when knocked to the ground while questioning a suspect at Golders Green.

1930
PC Arthur Lawes Fatally injured attempting to stop a stolen car being driven without lights at night in Tooting.

1931
PC George William Allen and PC Harry Cautherley Killed when their motorcycle combination crashed while pursuing a car at Beckenham.

PC William George Ware Drowned when his police motor patrol boat was struck by a steam tug and sank near Chiswick.

1933
PC Frederick William Percy Fatally injured on point duty in Chelsea when a cab collided with a lorry which fell onto him.

1934
PC James Robert Carter Fatally injured when knocked down by a motor car while on night point duty in Hampstead

1935
PC Henry Arthur Groves Fatally injured when thrown from his horse while attempting to avoid pedestrians in The Mall.

PC James Warrender Thomson KPM Struck and killed while trying to clear a crowd from the path of a lorry at Barnet Fair.

1937
SPS Frederick William Parncutt and PC Albert Arthur Taylor Drowned when their patrol boat was struck by a tug and sank near Poplar.

PC Bernard Tutt Fatally injured saving children from a vehicle, which mounted the pavement in Marylebone.

1938
PC George Thomas Shepherd Killed when thrown from the running board of a car, the driver of which he was seeking to stop in Hampstead.

1940
WRC Jack William Avery Stabbed and fatally wounded questioning a suspect near the gun emplacements in Hyde Park.

1943
PC Harry Pickett Killed when struck by a passing lorry while questioning a suspect in a vehicle at Banstead.

1944
PC Walter Charles Tralau Fatally injured on his beat at Chingford when his bicycle was hit by a vehicle in the blackout.

1947
PC Gilbert Edward Perkins and PC Leslie Edwin Thompson Both officers were killed when their wireless car crashed on an urgent call at Woodford.

1948
PC Nathanael Edgar Shot three times and fatally wounded by a suspect he was questioning at Winchmore Hill.

1952
PC Sidney George Miles KPFSM Shot in the head and killed while attempting to arrest armed suspects trapped on a roof in Croydon.

1954
PC Percy James Claxton Fatally injured in an explosion investigating a suspected suicide and gas escape at Hampstead.

1956
Sgt Leonard Alfred Demmon QPM Shot and killed by EOKA terrorists while seconded to the UK Police Unit in Cyprus.

T/Sgt Reginald William Tipple Shot and killed by an EOKA terrorist while seconded to the UK Police Unit in Cyprus.

1957
Supt Cornelius Carson Collapsed and died going to the assistance of a child after a fire at Hackney Police Station.

1958
PC Raymond Henry Summers Stabbed in the back and killed when he intervened in a street gang affray at night in Holloway.

1959
Detective Sgt Raymond William Purdy Shot dead while detaining a wanted man he had chased and arrested in South Kensington.

1960
PC Edward Roy Dorney Hit by a train and killed with his police dog while

tracking suspects on the railway at Deptford.

PC Leslie Edwin Vincent Meehan Run over and killed when a suspect in a car in Woolwich drove off with him on the side.

1961
SPS Frederick George Hutchins QPM and Insp Philip Pawsey QPM Both officers were shot and fatally wounded when pursuing and attempting to arrest an armed suspect who escaped from West Ham Police Station.

1966
PC Geoffrey Roger Fox, DS Christopher Tippett Head, and **TDC David Stanley Bertram Wombwell** All shot dead without warning as they questioned three suspects in a van at Shepherds Bush.

1967
PC Desmond Morgan Acreman Fatally injured when hit by a car while chasing suspected thieves across a road in Plumstead.

1971
PC Douglas Frederick Beckerson Killed in a fall through a glass roof when trying to arrest a violent suspect at Baker Street Station.

1973
PC Michael Anthony Whiting QPM Killed in Oxford Street when a suspect vehicle drove off and crashed as he clung to the side.

1975
PC Stephen Andrew Tibble QPM Fatally shot while off duty trying to stop a man being chased by colleagues in Hammersmith.

Explosives Officer Captain Roger Philip Goad GC BEM Killed by the explosion of a terrorist bomb, which he was attempting to defuse in Kensington.

1980
PC Francis Joseph O'Neill QGM Fatally stabbed when questioning a suspect whilst on plain clothes duty at Waterloo.

1981
Explosives Officer Kenneth Robert Howorth GM Killed in an explosion while attempting to defuse a terrorist bomb in a restaurant in Oxford Street.

1983
WPC Jane Philippa Arbuthnot, Inspector Stephen John Dodd and Sgt Noel Joseph Lane The three officers died from multiple injuries received while investigating a suspected terrorist car bomb in Knightsbridge when the device exploded.

1984
WPC Yvonne Joyce Fletcher Shot by terrorists and fatally wounded policing a political demonstration in St. James's Square.

PC Stephen John Jones Fatally injured when run down attempting to stop a drunk driver for speeding at Holloway.

1985
PC Keith Henry Blakelock QGM Brutally beaten and stabbed to death by a large mob during rioting at Tottenham.

DC John William Fordham Died from multiple stab wounds received when attacked whilst on surveillance duty in Kent.

1986
PC Martin Bell Killed when a drunk driver pursued by police in West Putney struck his unmarked car.

1987
PC Ronan Konrad Aidan McCloskey Killed when a drunk driver drove off with him clinging to the car and crashed at Willesden.

1989
PC Paul Maurice Breen Killed while navigating in an army ambulance, which crashed on an emergency in Camberwell.

1990
PC Laurence Peter Brown shot dead with a sawn-off shotgun as he approached a suspect in an ambush in Hackney.

PC Ashley Day Killed when the area car in which he was operator crashed while responding to an alarm in Acton.

1991
PC Robert Chenery Gladwell Died from injuries received when struck on the head while making an arrest in Paddington.

Sgt Alan Derek King Fatally wounded when a suspect he stopped at Walthamstow repeatedly stabbed him.

DC James Morrison QGM Fatally stabbed attempting to arrest a thief he had chased while off duty at Covent Garden.

1993
PC Patrick Dunne Shot dead when he confronted suspects while investigating the sound of gunfire in Clapham.

1994
Sgt Derek John Carnie Robertson QGM Fatally stabbed attempting to arrest an armed suspect at a robbery in New Addington.

1995
PC Phillip John Walters Shot and fatally wounded during a violent struggle to arrest a man at a disturbance in Ilford.

1997
WPC Nina Alexandra MacKay Stabbed and fatally wounded after forcing entry to a flat to arrest a wanted man in Stratford.

Index

Credits

The Metropolitan Police Service wishes to thank the following people who kindly gave their time and expertise during the production of this book:

Alison Tutton, Andrew Begg, Andy Baker, Angie Evans, Anna De Vries, Bill Griffiths, Bob Mackie, Carole Howlett, Caroline Kenyon, Chris Webb, Christopher White, Clare Baggaley, Dainis Ozols, Dan Maskell, Dave Chennell, Des Stout, Dick Fedorcio, Felicity Ross, Gary Mason, Gary Pugh, Graham Wettone, Guy Morgan, Hamish Campbell, Harry Whitehead, Jayme Johnson, Jenny Powell, John Bunn, John Coles, John Grieve, John Ross, John Sutherland, John Sweeney, Joy Bentley, Keith Asman, Keith Skinner, Lindsay Clutterbuck, Lorraine Homer, Luke Knight, Maggie Bird, Martin Tiplady, Mick Messinger, Mick Turner, Paul Begg, Paul Robinson, Penny Craig, Peter Clarke, Piers Murray Hill, Pippa Wadsworth, Ray Seal, Richard Farmery, Robert Proudfoot (London Fire Brigade), Ros Lavine, Ruth Shulver, Sara Cheesley, Sarah Edwards, Sarah Partridge, Simon Ovens, Simon Wilder, Stella Caldwell, Stephanie Day, Steve Allen, Steve Behan, Steve Mockett, Terry Jones (London Fire Brigade), Toby Harris, Tom Kerrigan, Tom Oakley, Tony Speed, Tristan Newkey-Burden, Vicky Holmes and Will O'Reilly.

The project co-ordinators wish to give special thanks to Maurice Garvie of the Fingerprint Bureau for his invaluable help with the book.

The publishers would like to thank the following sources for their kind permission to reproduce the pictures in the book:

All images kindly supplied by the Metropolitan Police Archive unless otherwise stated:

Corbis Images: 52–53, 82; /David Bebber/Reuters: 119, 150; /Brendan Beirne: 124; /Paul Hackett/Reuters: 144; /Hulton-Deutsch Collection: 40, 42, 94; /Peter Macdiarmid: 152; /Michael Nicholson: 6; /Reuters: 63, 115, 125; /Per Wilkund: 116

Getty Images: Central Press: 60; /Eric Fererberg/AFP: 56–57; /Hulton Archive: 13, 138–139; /Keystone: 87; /Reg Speller/Fox Photos: 123; /Steve Wood/Evening Standard: 97

Mary Evans Picture Library: 10–11, 14, 21

Rex Features: 8–9, 69, 74, 106, 111, 151; /Photo News Service: 112

Science Photo Library: Mauro Fermariello: 140

Every effort has been made to acknowledge correctly and contact the source and/or copyright holder of each picture. Carlton Books Limited apologises for any unintentional errors or omissions which will be corrected in future editions of this book.